Managers and Leaders Who Can

Managers and Leaders Who Can

How you survive and succeed in the new economy

Ruth Spellman

A John Wiley and Sons, Ltd, Publication

A catalogue record for this book is available from the British Library.

ISBN 978-1-119-99398-8 (hardback), ISBN 978-1-119-97783-4 (ebook)
ISBN 978-1-119-97784-1 (ebook), ISBN 978-1-119-97785-8 (ebook)

Typeset in 10pt ScalaOT by Sparks (www.sparkspublishing.com)
Printed in Great Britain by TJ International Ltd, Padstow, Cornwall.

CONTENTS

As Chief Executive of the Chartered Management Institute (CMI), Ruth Spellman OBE leads the drive to encourage greater focus on the high-level skills needed to build UK competitiveness and productivity. She is also responsible for the Institute's campaign to ensure that 50% of managers are professionally qualified by 2020.

Prior to joining the CMI in June 2008, Ruth served as the first female Chief Executive of the Institution of Mechanical Engineers (IMechE). She also spent seven years as Chief Executive of Investors in People (IIP), where she helped to raise the profile of the employer-led organisation across 27 countries. During this period she was appointed Chair of the skills body for the voluntary sector in a non-executive role, and was a Non-executive Director of Thompsons Solicitors.

As HR Director for the National Society for the Prevention of Cruelty to Children (NSPCC), Ruth was responsible for HR strategy, change management, resourcing strategy, employee communications, external communications and media relations. Her consultancy knowledge and strength resulted in new NSPCC policies that helped it to win the coveted Employer of the Year Award in 1996.

Ruth also spent five years working for Coopers & Lybrand. During this time, she worked with the boards of six of the UK's top 100 companies and set up one of the firm's HR branches.

In 2007, Ruth was awarded an OBE in the New Year Honours List for services to workplace learning. She was also recently voted 14th out of the 100 most influential HR individuals in the UK.

She has three grown-up children and currently resides in London.

ACKNOWLEDGEMENTS

I would like to thank all the contributors to the book for their time and wisdom. Many of them are distinguished Companions of the Chartered Management Institute, but all have had a substantial role in leading positions.

Their practical insights, knowledge born of experience and reflective approach to this project have helped me to look behind the headlines and the facade to the reality of management and leadership in the 2010s – messy, complicated, challenging, exciting and important. The vital ingredient in our ongoing competitive success.

I would also like to thank Erika Lucas, who has crafted the chapters, taking my ideas and making them intelligible; Claire Plimmer, who has been a guiding hand; Carol Anne Kaveney, Hannah Chapman and Analiza Gabuat, who have enabled this book to be written alongside many other priorities in the diary; and Tim Melville-Ross, whose idea it was that I should write this book.

Thank you.

Peter Ayliffe, President and Chief Executive of VisaEurope
Martin Bean, Vice Chancellor, The Open University
Lord Bichard, founder, Institute for Government
Lord Bilimoria, Chairman, Cobra Beer Partnership
Helen Brand, Chief Executive, Association of Chartered Certified Accountants (ACCA)
Rita Clifton, UK Chairman, Interbrand
Professor Cary Cooper, Lancaster University Management School
Penny de Valk, Chief Executive Officer, Institute of Leadership and Management (ILM)
Adrian Godfrey, Chair, Institute of Business Consulting and Partner, Ernst & Young
Steve Holliday, Chief Executive, National Grid
Sir David Howard, Chairman, Charles Stanley
Stephen Howard, Chief Executive, Business in the Community (BITC)
Paul Idzik, Chief Executive, DTZ Holdings plc
Sir Paul Judge, Chairman, Schroder Income Growth Fund
Sir Alan Langlands, Chief Executive, Higher Education Funding Council (HEFCE)
Rob Law, founder, Magmatic
Calvert Markham, Managing Director, Elevation Learning
Nigel Meager, Director, Institute for Employment Studies (IES)
Tim Melville-Ross, Group Chairman, DTZ Holdings plc
Terry Morgan, Chairman, Crossrail
Sir David Nicholson, Chief Executive, NHS

David Noble, Chief Executive, Chartered Institute of Purchasing and Supply (CIPS)

Vicky O'Dea, Operations Director, Serco

Jackie Orme, CEO, Chartered Institute of Personnel and Development (CIPD)

Jonathan Perks, global CEO leadership coach

Stefan Stern, Director of Strategy, Edelman

Andrew Summers, Chairman of the Steering Board, Companies House

Sir John Sunderland, former Non-executive Chairman, Cadbury Schweppes

Ed Sweeney, Chair, ACAS

John Taylor, Chief Executive, ACAS

Charles Tilley, Chief Executive, Chartered Institute of Management Accountants (CIMA)

Jill Tombs, Director of Human Resources and Governance, Mencap

Mark Turner, Senior Partner, GatenbySanderson

Phillippa Williamson, Chief Executive, Serious Fraud Office

When the CBI contributed to the *Leitch Review of Skills* in 2006, we said addressing the shortfall of management and leadership skills should be a national priority.

Although much has changed since then, this skills shortfall remains, and has the potential to hold back the economic recovery.

As Chartered Management Institute (CMI) data show, only one in five managers currently has a management qualification.

In this important book, Ruth Spellman highlights ways that this can be tackled, and how managers and leaders can develop their professional skills.

The practical insights from business leaders and many distinguished companions of the CMI provide an excellent guide to managers from any profession. They show how leadership roles are expanding and changing, and how issues like risk management, carbon emissions and, above all, ethics and values are becoming more and more important.

We now have higher expectations of fairness and openness, and we saw in the recession how improved communications were invaluable in holding off job losses, as better-informed staff had a clearer picture of their employer's business situation.

As we look for growth in the years ahead, managers and leaders need the right learning resources and positive role models to develop and refine their skills.

The CBI worked closely with Ruth Spellman when she led Investors in People, and so knows her views on better people management must be taken seriously.

So we welcome and recommend this book to managers and policy-makers alike, and hope it makes the contribution it deserves to in this critical debate.

John Cridland
CBI Director-General

I was talking recently to a manager who faced the challenge of reducing the headcount in his division by more than half. He was charged with making difficult decisions, in an extremely short timescale, about who should stay and who should go, and how the depleted team should be re-organised.

At the same time, the same manager was being presented with ever more ambitious growth targets for his division and was grappling with the dilemma of how to achieve better results with significantly fewer people and a dramatically reduced budget.

Sadly, this scenario is not uncommon. Times are tough and the role of leaders and managers has never been more challenging. This book has been written in recognition of the fact that, more than ever before, managers need to reinforce their confidence and competence by accessing practical help and advice to negotiate their way through the turbulent, fast-moving business climate.

Technological change, growing consumer power and an unprecedented level of global competition means the pace of change has accelerated to an alarming degree. Managers now have to run simply to stay still and have no time to even catch their breath before the next wave of change comes crashing in.

We need to recognise that today's managers are also operating in uncharted territory. The rules have changed and many of the old certainties no longer exist. The established truth about good behaviour being rewarded and bad behaviour being punished, for example, seems to have disappeared. Recent experience has shown that even when those at the helm of organisations make catastrophic decisions, they are still rewarded handsomely and appear not to be held accountable for their actions.

Our members at the Chartered Management Institute (CMI) tell us that such an atmosphere leaves them feeling lost and in the dark. They need guidance about how to behave, practical help with the seemingly endless stream of challenges presented to them and the opportunity to find out how their peers in other sectors and organisations are coping.

Above all, they need help in understanding how a values-driven, ethical approach to business can help them emerge from the maelstrom with their organisation in good shape and their heads held high.

Young managers in the lower and middle ranks of organisations are particularly vulnerable as we attempt to negotiate our way slowly and painfully out of recession. They have only known the good times and do not necessarily have the more sophisticated level of skills required to manage against the backdrop of a challenging economic climate.

At a time when budgets are being squeezed to the limit, there is a tendency for organisations to cut back on management training and development. This is both short-sighted and counter-productive. It means that managers, particularly those in the earlier stages of their career, are left exposed and that the ability of the business to improve performance and meet future challenges is stymied.

Now, more than ever, organisations should be building managerial capability and making sure their people are well equipped enough to drive and manage change, and exploit new opportunities.

The management job has become more complex, encompassing everything from managing policy, stakeholders and environmental impact to managing brand, reputation, change and innovation. Managers also need to adjust to increased transparency, the world of 'WikiLeaks' and the growing public appetite for increased accountability.

In this book I have interviewed some of today's leading figures from the public and private sector. They have a wealth of experience and wisdom to share on some of the most pressing issues facing those at the helm of today's organisations.

In writing this book, I have been influenced by their views, by the research and evidence to which the Chartered Management Institute has access, and by my own gut instincts. Although we live in hard times, we have a thousand opportunities a day to do things better by being proactive. Managing risks, seizing opportunities and becoming better at stakeholder management are realistic aspirations for us all.

The CMI also has a wealth of experience to draw on, and this book provides an opportunity for us to share some of our latest cutting edge research and thinking. We hope all managers find it a useful resource and a stimulant to their thinking.

Ruth Spellman
CEO, Chartered Management Institute

CHAPTER 1

Ethics and values are critical. Business can no longer get by saying one thing and doing another.

Jackie Orme, CEO, Chartered Institute of Personnel and Development

Values and ethics have a vital role to play in the modern business world. Leaders and managers are faced with an increasingly complex and challenging business environment. They are battling to keep up with the pace of technological change, struggling to fend off growing competition and grappling with a difficult economic climate.

In the midst of this maelstrom, a strong set of values can serve to illuminate the way ahead. They are the foundation for strong leadership and management, the glue that sticks the organisation together and the unwritten code that helps managers make the right decisions about what they do and how they do it. Values help employees make sense of the new and constantly changing challenges they are being asked to take on and give them a clear picture of how the organisation wants them to behave.

There are some high-profile examples of organisations that have achieved outstanding results by putting values at the heart of everything they do. Virgin and Pret A Manger, for example, are both highly successful businesses with a distinctive, ethical approach. This is not just tokenism, but a deep-seated ethos that permeates both organisations. Virgin, for example, places huge emphasis across its operations on being a responsible service provider, managing its impact on the environment and playing a role in the communities that it operates in. Pret A Manger has a strong tradition of developing its people, places a high value on encouraging diversity and actively raises funds and donates products to charities for the homeless across the UK.

The truth, however, is that many organisations are still struggling to get to grips with how they can effectively harness the power of values on an ongoing basis. They may well have a glossy values statement pinned to the wall in their corporate HQ, but their employees are not living and breathing those values on a day-to-day basis.

The pages of the national press are full of examples of what happens when organisations fail to approach business from an ethical standpoint – or when the actions they take are not congruent with the values they pretend to espouse.

Reputations that have taken years to build can be damaged by a succession of unfortunate media headlines. BP is the latest in a long line of examples from the corporate world. It is estimated that damage done to the business as a result of the Gulf of Mexico oil spill could result in losses of up to £15 billion. The recent MP expenses scandal in the UK, where MPs were exposed for unethical charging of expenses, has also graphically illustrated the importance that people attach to following a moral code rather than simply obeying the rules.

But what do we really mean when we talk about values? How do leaders and managers develop values propositions that support their business objectives? What do they need to do to ensure their employees buy into those values and demonstrate them in their dealings with stakeholders on a daily basis?

Leader insights

Ethics and values are absolutely essential for a successful business. Leaders must accept that they are being watched all the time. Businesses should not complain about transparency – they must deal with it.

Steve Holliday, Chief Executive, National Grid

Recession has reinforced the need for sharing values – to overcome adversity and build back faith in the future.

Lord Bichard, founder, Institute for Government

Ethics and values have a central role. You need to be transparent in your decision-making and exercise a clear sense of propriety. You should have your limits, beyond which you will not go.

Phillippa Williamson, Chief Executive, Serious Fraud Office

Perception versus intent

It's important to recognise that most organisations do actually go about their business with honourable intent. Yes, they are there to make a profit and provide a good return for their shareholders, but they don't generally set out to rip people off, damage the environment or have a negative impact on the communities they operate in.

Despite their good intentions, however, organisations tend to get a pretty poor press. The media are quick to jump onto any misdemeanour and to bay for the blood of the leaders involved, even if there was no malicious intent or serious operational failing.

Trust and respect for business leaders themselves – with a few notable exceptions – is also generally low. Indeed, surveys have shown that business leaders come second from bottom, just above politicians, in terms of public regard.

This negative perception is not just external – it's often prevalent inside organisations too. Endless rounds of cuts and re-organisations have left employees feeling insecure, initiative-weary and, frankly, pretty cynical about the businesses they work for.

Organisations such as the Chartered Institute of Personnel and Development (CIPD) have been warning for some time that a lack of employee engagement is one of the biggest issues facing the corporate world right now. On the front line, the troops are becoming weary and are feeling disconnected with the battles they are being asked to fight. 'We're all in this together', even if it is true, has a somewhat hollow ring.

In this scenario, values are the secret weapon. They can help organisations protect their reputation and improve the way they are perceived by the outside world. Values can create cohesion within the business, ensure everyone is working towards the same goal and help employees make that all-important personal connection with the tasks they are being asked to perform.

The right time – or all the time?

The V word has a tendency to rise to the top of the organisational agenda when things are going badly. It's often a bit of a knee-jerk reaction. The top team need something that will quickly bind the business together after a merger; HR want to re-energise people following a significant downsizing exercise; managers need an intervention that will help them focus on priorities and deliver their business objectives in a difficult climate.

There's nothing wrong with taking a fresh look at values at times of significant change and difficulty. They can play a valuable role when there's an urgent need to boost morale, accelerate change or respond to a new business challenge. It's not necessary, however, to wait for the worst-case scenario. Becoming a values-driven organisation is an approach that's equally relevant in good times and bad. A values-driven approach can help keep the business on an even keel when times are good and can even help it get better at what it does.

It's not about responding to a crisis with a quick fix. It's about setting the tone, establishing the ground rules, making it clear 'how we do things around here' and ensuring that employees know what kind of behaviours will be recognised and rewarded.

It's also important to recognise that becoming a values-driven organisation is not a one-off event. The business world never stands still; as the sands shift around them, organisations need to review their values constantly to make sure they are still fit for purpose. This doesn't mean starting all over again – it's just a case of recognising that the business may need to tweak the values occasionally to make sure they still fit the bill.

The stringent savings being demanded of the public sector right now are a case in point. As budgets are slashed, significant changes will have to be made to the way services are designed, packaged and delivered.

Values will provide the guidelines to make sure organisations act responsibly and in the best interests of the people they serve when they are faced with difficult decisions.

Leader insights

Ethics and values are right at the heart of any great management and leadership team.

Martin Bean, Vice Chancellor, The Open University

Ethics and values are absolutely critical to every successful business. In Magmatic, I have asked all my team to draw how they see the company values and to display these pictures in their own work areas. Somehow the visual representation really helps them understand the values that are most important in our culture.

Rob Law, founder, Magmatic

I believe ethics and values are critical to business, a bit like oxygen is essential to life. It's not about being puritanical, it's about inspiring trust, particularly during difficult or hard times.

Jonathan Perks, Global CEO Leadership Coach

Consultation, not coercion

The big question facing many organisations is how they go about defining what they stand for and what their values really are.

There's a tendency for leaders and managers to spend hours closeted in boardrooms trying to thrash out some kind of statement that resonates with all. When the discussion and debate are over, what often happens is that a list of agreed values is printed on cards and posters and launched with much fanfare to the waiting staff.

The problem is that this kind of approach just doesn't work, because values can't simply be decided by the chosen few and imposed from on high. An organisation will only get buy-in to its values if they are developed in consultation with the people who will have to implement them on a daily basis and with the stakeholders who will be on the receiving end.

Organisations need to think about what they want to achieve, how they plan to get there, what messages they want to convey to the outside world and what obstacles might get in the way. They need to invite contributions and feedback from everyone involved and gradually paint a picture of what makes the organisation tick, what needs to be done differently and what customers and stakeholders really want.

The most effective values statements are likely to be those that build on existing strengths and tackle areas of difficulty head on. They need to be intrinsically linked with the organisation's strategic objectives and fully endorsed and espoused by the top team.

Leader insight

What we are seeing is a broad shift in culture. We are seeing a global push towards more accountability. People need to make judgements all the time, but they need to be able to justify them. We need to enable business executives to be accountable and robust.

Paul Idzik, Chief Executive, DTZ Holdings plc

Living the values

If values are going to make it off the piece of paper and into something that becomes an integral part of how the organisation does business, they need to be communicated to employees in a way that makes it clear what they are required to do.

There's a tendency for organisations to describe their values in quite sweeping, general terms. 'Our people are our most important asset', 'We strive for continuous improvement' and 'We respect diversity' are the kinds of phrases that are often bandied around. These are all very laudable statements, but the problem is it's not clear to employees what they might need to do differently when they come to work on Monday morning.

In the command and control regimes of the past, this wouldn't have been a problem. Managers issued very specific directives and employees did exactly what they were told. It's now widely acknowledged that these old management styles just don't work in the new world. In the fast-moving, technology-driven, global reality of business today, organisations expect – and indeed need – their employees to take the initiative, respond rapidly, seize opportunities and deliver what the customer wants.

Leaders need their people to be fully engaged with what the organisation is trying to achieve so that they will generate the new ideas that will take the business forward and will be willing to go the extra mile when required.

As a manager, when you are creating your values statements, you should consider making them much more explicit so that they provide real guidance to the employee on the front line about how they are expected to behave in pursuit of the targets and challenges they have been set. Statements like 'We always go one step further for the customer', for example, would help employees connect in a much more meaningful way with a customer service-related value.

This more direct expression of values gives employees a shared purpose, a common goal and a benchmark against which to measure their behaviour. It provides a clear indication of the actions that will be rewarded and gives managers a framework for dealing with behaviour that is inconsistent with the values, should it arise.

Demonstrating that values are at the very core of the business and driving actions and decisions is a key requirement of the Investors in People (IIP) standard. To be awarded IIP status, organisations need to show that they are taking a values-led approach and that managers and employees within the business truly understand what this means and are applying it to their work.

Assessors explore whether this is the case through interviews with employees and by demonstration of evidence against some key criteria.

The following indicators of good practice, taken from the IIP framework, can help organisations judge how far down the road they are to becoming an authentic values-driven business.

- Top managers make sure the organisation has a clear set of core values that support its purpose and vision.
- Top managers make sure the core values are at the heart of the organisation's strategy and govern the way it operates.
- Managers can describe the organisation's core values and what this means to the way they are expected to manage.
- Managers can describe how they make sure the core values are at the heart of the way that the organisation operates.
- People can describe the organisation's core values and what this means to the way they are expected to work.
- People believe in and share the organisation's vision and values.
- Managers can describe how they play an important role in recruiting and selecting people with values that match the organisation's values.
- Top managers can describe how they define the current and future capabilities managers need in line with the organisation's purpose, vision and values.
- Top managers can describe how they act as role models when demonstrating the leadership and management capabilities in line with the organisation's values.
- Managers can describe how they lead, manage and develop people in line with the organisation's values.
- People can describe how their manager leads, manages and develops them in line with the organisation's values.

(© Investors in People, UK Commission for Employment and Skills, www.investorsinpeople.co.uk.)

Personal values and ethics

As a manager, it is of paramount importance that you understand the connection between the personal values of the individual and the values adopted by the organisation they work for. Employees will only buy into corporate values if they can see how those values align with their own personal value set. To take an extreme example, a virulent anti-smoker wouldn't feel comfortable working for a tobacco company.

The mismatch isn't always quite so obvious. There can be more subtle nuances around the qualities that an organisation might hold dear among its managers – a hard-nosed, commercial, thrusting approach, for example – and the way that an individual might prefer to go about their work.

The reality is that in many cases where this occurs, individuals will 'self-select' and make a decision to leave. This is not necessarily a negative – someone who is deeply uncomfortable with the way an organisation goes about its business is unlikely to perform well anyway, regardless of how talented they might be. It is when the values of the individual are a close match with the values of the organisation that people perform at their peak.

Many of the leaders who have contributed to this book have talked about how strong personal values are at the root of their effectiveness in their role. As a good leader, you truly have to wear your values on your sleeve, because before people will follow you, they have to be clear about what you stand for.

One example is Peter Ayliffe, President and Chief Executive of VisaEurope, who believes strongly in the importance of openness and trust between managers and leaders and the workforce. He has personally dedicated a great deal of time and effort to make the strategy of Visa a document that is well-thumbed and easy to read and access. Aligning individual and organisational objectives really helps the organisation to succeed and creates a win–win situation. His views on the importance of ethics and values are that: 'Nothing is more important. You can't be a leader without qualities of integrity and honesty. Short-term pressures make these values even more important.'

At Cadbury, the ethos and values of the Cadbury family endured long after the company became public. The care of employees in the provision of housing, welfare and education, in addition to employment and the general concern for all stakeholders, remained in the company's genetic structure. In the modern company there was a strong sense of straightforwardness in communication, of honesty being the best policy. Politics were not part of the culture and long-term thinking versus short-term expediency was encouraged. 'Cadbury values pervaded the business and underwrote employee loyalty and the culture of long service,' explained Sir John Sunderland, until 2008 the Non-executive Chairman of Cadbury Schweppes.

Sir John describes a strong cultural fit with his own ideas on management and leadership. He believes in doing any job to the fullest extent of one's ability and feels this can apply to any generation or individual. Without this level of commitment, work is less satisfying and perhaps progress more limited.

When the path gets tough, the importance of strong values and shared beliefs cannot be overstated. It's what binds people together and keeps the wheels turning when everything comes crashing down around you.

The most graphic recent illustration of this was the ability of the Chilean mine shift supervisor Luis Urzua to provide strong leadership for his men during their long incarceration underground. The belief and respect the miners held for him meant he was able to maintain control, keep hope alive and spirits high, particularly during the dark days before there was any contact with the outside world. He maintained his strong values-driven approach to the very end by volunteering to be the last one out.

Of course it's not just during the bad times that you have to demonstrate as a leader a strong personal value set. It's important in good times too that you behave in a way that is consistent and upholds and reflects the ideals on which the business operates.

Leader insights

Values should underlie your actions. You cannot then fail yourself.
Sir John Sunderland, former Non-executive Chairman, Cadbury
Schweppes

Ethics are absolutely critical. You can't lead without trust and integrity. Increasingly, the market values integrity as well as profitability.
Penny de Valk, Chief Executive Officer, Institute of Leadership
and Management (ILM)

Values in the public sector

Values and ethics play an even more important role in the public sector, where the emphasis is on delivering a service rather than the bottom line.

According to long-time civil servant Lord Bichard, it is often ad-herence to values that is one of the primary motivations for talented individuals choosing to work in the public sector. Recent events have undoubtedly drawn attention to the importance of values provided they are 'real' and not just espoused.

'Often in the public sector there is a gap between aspiration and result – frustration sets in, which can of course be counter-productive. Managers in the public sector must adapt and change; keep their values, but but be flexible about virtually everything else,' he says.

While managers and leaders in the public sector and private sectors need access to the same skills, the private sector is less overtly politi-cal and may feel less accountable for values and behaviours. 'Against this, little gestures from leaders can make a massive difference. Per-sonal acknowledgement, saying thank you, being open to challenge and management by walking about are not just questions of style – they can make a substantial difference,' explains Lord Bichard.

The public sector is under unprecedented pressure to cut costs. Managers will face difficult decisions about what stays and what goes, and will have to find new and innovative ways of delivering services. Some of these decisions will be unpopular and there is a danger that employees may start to feel demoralised and under siege.

Values will play a key role in helping managers make appropriate choices and ensuring the needs of some of the most vulnerable sections of society continue to be met.

The public sector has, of course, always been populated by people who want to give back to society and make a difference. The desire to do something meaningful underpins the whole purpose of the public service being provided, whether it is in the field of defence, education, health or public utilities such as transport and energy.

High degrees of trust are vested in the managers and leaders of essential public services; however, very little is made these days of the concept of 'public service'. Perhaps it is due for a renaissance as David Cameron's 'Big Society' idea begins to crystallise.

Cameron's vision is to encourage more 'people power', giving communities and individuals the support and resources to run some of their own local projects and services. Early pilot projects have included local buy-out of a rural pub, recruitment of volunteers to keep museums open and giving residents more say over public spending.

There has been some cynicism that this is just a euphemism for less public investment or another way of reducing the tax burden on the working population. It will be interesting to watch the experiment develop and to see if communities respond to the challenge. The evidence certainly suggests that people are highly motivated to volunteer, particularly when it has a direct impact on the area they live in or on projects that they have a personal interest or stake in.

Clearly, political views vary about the way public goods and services should be funded, or indeed managed – but the idea that we will always need to produce and consume them is not in dispute. The story of how success in public service delivery will be measured in the future, however, is still unfolding.

The evaluation of how services are provided is partly economic but also partly a reflection of our social and political values. In the past, success has often been measured to a large degree in financial terms, but we are now moving towards a deeper understanding of the social cost benefit of our goods and services. As the new face of public service begins to emerge, we are likely to see less emphasis on searching for the lowest cost provider and more focus on measuring the real social outcomes on the ground.

As this approach becomes more prevalent, we will hopefully see more longer-term contracts being awarded that take into account the bigger picture of the social and economic benefits to everyone involved.

Case study: Using values to drive prison service reform

The work done by Serco at Doncaster Prison and Youth Offenders Institute is an excellent illustration of how values can be used to drive improved performance and better social outcomes.

Serco is one of the world's leading service and outsourcing companies. It has contracts with a wide range of local authorities and public sector organisations, and delivers services across justice and healthcare to education and defence on their behalf.

The business currently employs 70 000 people, is a member of the FTSE 100 and has a corporate vision of becoming one of the top 750 global companies by 2020.

For the past 16 years, Serco has been responsible for the management of HMP and YOI Doncaster – a category 'B' remand centre in South Yorkshire that holds up to 1145 remand or sentenced male prisoners over the age of 18. There are 600 staff who provide cover 24/7, 365 days a year.

The prison's vision is to promote innovative solutions to produce significant benefits for the prisoners, their families and the communities of South Yorkshire. It has won a number of awards, including the Charter Mark for excellence in the provision of public services, and has been described as being 'among the best' local prisons for resettlement and outreach support for prisoners and their families.

HMP Doncaster has, however, faced a number of challenges in recent years – highlighted by prison inspection reports that identified a number of significant weaknesses. It was rated at Performance Level 2 (Level 4 is the highest, Level 1 the lowest). Staff morale was low and there was a high turnover of first-line managers at the start of their prison management careers. Other areas of weakness highlighted by the report included an increase in incidents of violence and self-harm, and a lack of purposeful activity for prisoners.

John Biggin, director of HMP and YOI Doncaster, explains the challenges he faced when he joined Doncaster in 2010:

The inspection reports had highlighted some shortcomings at Doncaster and we realised that overcoming these issues would require a high level of strategic planning from our managers. Direction from prison management needs to be strong, with a clear vision and set of values. To change Doncaster into a successful, high-performing prison, we needed to get the best out of every single manager on our team, at every level.

We knew the key areas for improvement in the prison, and we had to ensure our managers were in a position to take on these issues independently and come up with solutions to bring about change.

Biggin decided to use CMI training to help managers respond to issues at Doncaster more flexibly and imaginatively, and he encouraged them to put their ideas into practice and to 'make a difference'.

Some managers at HMP Doncaster were already working towards CMI qualifications, but a decision was taken to open the training up to all management staff, providing them with increased opportunities for professional and career development.

As the training progressed, staff morale and confidence grew as they started to apply what they were learning to the workplace, and began to think more strategically about how to overcome challenges.

This led to a number of innovative changes to help reduce re-offending. This included putting on a play for prisoners' children to help form closer bonds between families. A printing workshop was also introduced, with the dual purpose of employing and developing the skills of around 50 inmates while also meeting the needs of the local community.

The effect on performance has clearly been felt. HMP and YOI Doncaster recently moved from Level 2 to Level 3 in the scale of prison performance – a significant step that John Biggin credits to his management team.

> *I gave my managers some extremely challenging briefs to improve standards. CMI's management training has encouraged them to think outside the box and to feel less constrained by the way things have always been done. We've had to be creative and come up with ways to improve standards on a lean budget. There is now a real belief among the management team here that no job is too hard for them.*

This case illustrates the importance of reflecting social values and measuring social outcomes when projects or services are outsourced to private providers. Providers such as Serco must subscribe to the ethos of crime prevention – in the widest possible sense – if they are to be successful not only in reducing the prison population but in creating models of rehabilitation for ex-prisoners and offenders that actually work.

The social benefits of the approach taken at Doncaster are very clear, although as yet unquantified. However, we do know that it costs more money to keep someone in prison than to send them to university. In particular, if the case of Doncaster could be replicated, prisoners can learn and earn a living wage in prison while also contributing goods and services to the community. They can also lead worthwhile, self-supporting lives as soon as they come out. Through being integrated with their families during their period of incarceration, they are also able to regain their own self-respect.

Even somewhat cynical hardened criminals, as well as prison warders who have worked for many years in the prison service, have been impressed by the success of the Doncaster experiment and are convinced that many of the lessons are applicable elsewhere.

Making the link to CSR

Many organisations seek to demonstrate their values to the outside world through corporate social responsibility policies (CSR) or initiatives.

Definitions of exactly what CSR encompasses vary, but put simply, it's the deliberate inclusion of the wider public interest in corporate decision-making. Companies that place a strong emphasis on CSR measure their success against what is often referred to as the 'triple bottom line' – people, planet and profit.

So a CSR-focused business would proactively encourage the growth and development of the communities that it affects or operates within. It would also look to voluntarily eliminate practices that might harm the planet or have a negative impact on consumers, regardless of whether those practices were legal and profit-generating or not.

UK company law now requires organisations to provide information on their CSR initiatives in their annual report to shareholders. There is also now a recognised international standard for CSR (ISO 260000).

The CSR agenda has been driven to a large degree by consumers, who are increasingly demanding that organisations take a more ethical approach to business. People have become more aware of the environmental and social implications of their actions, and are beginning to think much more closely about what they buy, where they go and what activities they engage in.

Thanks to the explosion in online news and Internet discussion forums, consumers also now have much more opportunity to publicly voice their concerns about any organisational behaviour that they perceive to be unethical. Organisational misdemeanours that in the past may never have been uncovered can now be in the glare of the media spotlight very quickly.

The business case for CSR

It should be recognised that CSR is not just about establishing ethical credentials and creating a corporate glow of satisfaction. There is a strong business case for adhering to the triple bottom line, with multiple pay-offs for organisations.

An ethical approach to business can help organisations recruit and retain the talented employees that will drive their future growth. Research conducted by the Chartered Management Institute (*Generation Y: Unlocking the Talent of Young Managers*) shows that the emerging generation of managers place a strong emphasis on working environment and values. In the survey, 90% of respondents agreed that they wanted to work for an organisation that did something they believed in, regardless of whether it was in the public or private sector. Just over half (56%) said they would only work for an organisation that had strong values.

A genuine culture of 'doing the right thing' can also help to offset risks and lessen the likelihood of corruption scandals or environmental accidents. Would the MP expenses fiasco in the UK have happened if MPs had placed more value on acting appropriately rather than following the rules?

A strong emphasis on CSR can also help to build customer loyalty. The Body Shop and The Co-operative Group are examples of businesses that have made an ethical approach an integral part of their brand. Organisations that take a socially responsible approach will also reap the rewards in terms of improved employee engagement. Impact International is a consultancy that brings together corporate and community partners. In a recent edition of the CMI's magazine *Professional Manager*, MD Andy Dickson points out that 'employees are people who have interests outside of work and strong values, and they do things in their own time because they are passionate about them. If they are able to work with the community at work as well, it taps into their personal motivators, creates a bond between the employee and the business, and makes them proud to be part of an ethical organisation.'

There is inevitably some cynicism about the growing emphasis on CSR. Some critics claim that organisations engage in these initiatives to distract the public from ethical questions posed by their core operations. There's a suspicion that their motives are not entirely altruistic and they don't always 'walk the talk'. Some may claim they are committed to sustainable development, for example, while at the same time engaging in harmful business practices.

The debate about whether government and regulatory enforcement would be better than voluntary measures in ensuring that companies behave in a socially responsible manner will no doubt continue. As a leader, what you need to bear in mind is that unless CSR activities are purposeful, they won't be sustainable.

They also need to be rooted in genuine care and concern for the wider community. Thanks to the Internet there is nowhere to hide: organisations who fail to live up to their promises and pronouncements will soon be uncovered. Consumer confidence in the business will plummet and those valuable Generation Y employees will vote with their feet. The CMI's research clearly showed that if organisations failed to live up to their values and the claims made during recruitment, talented young individuals would quickly start to look elsewhere.

CSR in practice

Organisations put their CSR policies into practice in a number of ways. Some take a philanthropic approach, donating money to local organisations or giving aid to impoverished communities. This is very laudable, but it doesn't help to build the skills of the local people or improve their lives over the longer term.

Voluntary sector practitioners tell us they would like to see organisations looking beyond just giving money to projects that will then die without further funding. A more sustainable approach might be to set up 'evergreen' funds, where donations are reinvested and payments continue to do good year after year.

A more common approach is for corporations to work directly with local communities and voluntary organisations, to help them build skills and improve themselves. *Professional Manager* has recently reported on a number of such projects, ranging from bankers helping to construct a local adventure playground to managers acting as mentors for prisoners who are coming up for release and need support rebuilding their lives.

The idea of a 'time bank' appeals to many of the large companies that CMI comes into contact with – that is, they make their own talent available as a resource to help local charities develop expertise in areas such as HR, marketing, IT or finance. KPMG is one organisation that has been successfully using this approach for some time.

Other organisations have found ways to engage less senior employees in CSR activities too. A good example of this is the Reading for Schools programme, where junior staff are encouraged to work with local schools on a regular basis, helping pupils who may be struggling with their reading.

There is also an increasing trend to link CSR activities directly to organisational learning and development. Businesses are constantly looking for new and efficient ways to develop their staff and are realising that they can bring about a 'win-win' situation if they couple this with opportunities to partner with the social sector. Managers who are developing their marketing expertise, for example, might be charged with going into a charity and helping it overhaul its promotional materials. Fledgling executives who need project management experience could be given the task of developing a new IT infrastructure for a voluntary organisation.

Managed well, these kinds of initiatives can reap enormous rewards for everyone involved. The key is to find a compatible partner that the organisation can work comfortably with over time. Projects need to be carefully chosen and planned so that they meet the needs of the charity and deliver the desired learning outcomes for the organisation involved.

What makes these CSR initiatives work so well is that we are digging deep into the human psyche. At the CMI itself, it is great to see many of our employees' natural instinct to be generous, giving time as well as money to charitable causes. When asked why they do this, the answer often comes down to a personal story: the recipient is worthy, well-known in the locality of CMI's offices in Corby, or a member of staff has a relative who currently needs a vital service.

The National Council for Voluntary Organisations (NCVO) estimates that as many as one in five of us is currently a volunteer, demonstrating that people are very motivated to do something altruistic and give back to society.

As a leader or manager, you need to find ways of channelling this enthusiasm and energy for getting involved. Managed carefully, it can help to create a feel-good factor, fuel new ideas at work and develop new skills that the individual can bring back to their work.

Social entrepreneurship

Of course, socially responsible approaches don't have to just be add-ons to other corporate activities – they are quickly moving into the mainstream and becoming an alternative business model.

Many businesses are now set up purely as social enterprises, trading to generate income that is 'put back' into society rather than existing purely to create wealth for their shareholders. The Fifteen restaurants founded by Jamie Oliver, *The Big Issue* and the fair trade chocolate company Divine Chocolate are among the best-known examples.

There are also micro-credit businesses, such as the Grameen Bank, set up by Professor Muhammad Yunus. The bank has loaned more than $8.86 billion to 8.1 million borrowers, 97% of whom are women, to help build 640 000 homes. It has also sponsored more than 50 000 scholarships and student loans, and changed the lives of hundreds of Bangladeshi families (www.grameen-info.org).

There are in fact around 62 000 social enterprises in the UK, operating across a wide range of sectors. Health and social care is the largest category of trading activity, followed by education. Renewable energy, transport, recycling and fair trade are other common markets, although social enterprises can be successful in almost any sector. Already these organisations have a combined turnover of at least £27 billion, accounting for 5% of all businesses with employees and contributing £8.4 billion per year to the UK economy.

The difficult economic climate has presented real opportunities for these social enterprises. Increasing pressure on public sector spending means the government is constantly looking for new and effective ways to deliver mainstream services. As budgets dwindle, it is predicted that many local authorities will increasingly look to outsource services. Social enterprises, which often have their roots in the heart of local communities, will be ideal partners.

Business commentators have suggested that the social enterprise 'way' of doing business could soon become the norm rather than the exception to the rule. So a business that is struggling, for example, could be repacked into a social enterprise model, where the emphasis is perhaps on providing employment in a disadvantaged area rather than on purely making profits for shareholders. Or a company that manufactures soap might have employing visually impaired people as one of its key objectives. Danish IT firm Specialisterne is another good example of how social needs can sit at the heart of a business. The firm's business concept centres on using the special skills of people with autistic spectrum disorder (ASD). It tests software and conducts quality controls for companies such as Siemens, Microsoft, Cisco and CSC. In her book *The New Pioneers* (Wiley, 2010), Tania Ellis describes how the company's social business model was so successful that it became a Harvard Business School case study just four years after its inception. Founder Thorkil Sonne's long-term goal is to create one million jobs worldwide for people with ASD and similar challenges, and to change society's view of people with this disorder.

Funds are being set up to encourage this kind of approach – and although it is early days, the results are promising. Community Action Network Chief Executive Andrew Croft says: 'I think there could well be a time when every major corporate organisation is running a social business alongside its existing business, using its skills to create significant social value. There are some huge opportunities, which will also help mainstream businesses achieve far greater social credentials.'

Croft points out that when companies start to look at taking a more socially responsible approach, they often realise it can be a route to business transformation.

Take the example of the waste management company that started looking at ways to increase recycling. It found a way of turning some of its waste into a soil conditioning product that could be sold to garden centres. It has since gone on look at how it could produce energy from the by-products of its waste. So by trying to take a more environmentally friendly approach, it has been able to identify new products and income streams.

Board directors who are looking for the next source of innovation might be well placed to look at the CSR section of their annual reports and see if there is something in there that could transform the way they do business.

Graham Bann, Executive Director, Talent & Skills, Business in the Community (BITC), believes that CSR is not just a two-way street where corporates and individuals benefit; it is starting to redefine the way business is done and to redefine business itself in terms of social and cultural community objectives.

CSR helps to overcome tunnel vision in companies and get managers out of the silo mentality. It also helps aspirant leaders tap into their emotional intelligence and develop a rapport with staff and customers that is durable. At BITC, Graham Bann is passionate about another way of doing business – engaging with the community to deliver a better outcome. He sees the power of business mentoring on a daily basis. He has also witnessed major changes in CEOs as a result of their community involvement.

Marks & Spencer Chairman Sir Stuart Rose gave his personal support to 'work inspiration', which helps businesses provide meaningful and valuable work experience for young people. Steve Holliday at National Grid is never more relaxed than when he is working with BITC, involving National Grid employees in community projects and providing first-rate development opportunities for unemployed young people.

We still have a long way to go to make sure we use the whole talent pool, and both Sir Stuart Rose and Steve Holliday have become sensitive to and proactive on this issue as a result of their BITC involvement.

Support from professional bodies

With the recent spate of government cuts to the quangos, we will rely more on professional bodies to set standards and ensure that they are met.

As bodies such as the Financial Services Authority (FSA) are reformed, there are hopes that there will be more emphasis on the skills, competencies and values of those who are entrusted to make decisions. We may then have more real accountability in the system. No one can be held accountable for breaches of trust unless we are more explicit about the ethical code itself and make it a requirement, for example, for big financial institutions to uphold and enforce ethical behaviour.

It is in the interests of all businesses that we do 'good business' and that some of the excesses of recent years are not quickly reinstated. This is the inspiration behind a recently established body called Professions for Good, which represents professional bodies and is fundamentally concerned with more effective standard-setting.

Of course, throughout the professional bodies you have the issue of who represents our managers and leaders? What code are they following? When no one is looking, how do we make managers and leaders accountable for ethical management and leadership behaviour and practices?

Professional codes of conduct are perhaps a better way of regulating than the box-ticking approach where people become frightened to exercise independent judgement. One hopes that by encouraging people to use their own sense of right and wrong, advised and supported by a professional body, some errors of judgement could be avoided altogether. This also means that where errors are made, corrective action can be taken.

The CMI has responded to these issues with the introduction of the CMI Code. The code encapsulates what the Institute and its members stand for in terms of their professional conduct, behaviour and ethics. All members sign up to it on joining and reaffirm their commitment annually. The overall ethos of the code is captured in the following statement:

As a professional manager and member of the CMI, I will behave with honesty and integrity in my own actions as a manager and in my interactions with colleagues, my employing organisation, those with whom I come into contact in fulfilling my management role, the wider community and the Institute.

The code sets a high standard and the CMI provides support and advice to members as they seek to follow it in their personal management practice and their management of others. It also sets out their responsibilities to the organisation that employs them, their duty to deal appropriately with customers, suppliers and other stakeholders, and the way they should approach their dealings with the wider community.

The CMI would like to see the code included in the management and leadership development courses delivered at universities, colleges and business schools, and hopes that it will also be embraced by employers and other professional bodies. The CMI believes that the code should also be included in public-sector commissioning processes and should equally be applied to the consultancy profession. The vision is that professionalism in management should become much more widely accepted and practised, and that it should increasingly mean something to everyone.

The CMI is involved in other initiatives that will also support organisations in taking a more values-driven approach. It has been involved in researching and developing tools, for example, to assist organisations in implementing CSR.

One example of this is the work done in partnership with Business in the Community to add a management and leadership aspect to their BITC index. The existing BITC index measures the extent to which organisations are investing in CSR activities; the CMI believes that it is important they also measure the management and leadership capability that will support these initiatives, and has worked with them to develop an appropriate benchmarking tool.

The future

Trust and confidence march together and the capitalist economy depends on a large number of people trusting each other. This fundamental of business life is unlikely to change and will be a critical factor in getting the economies of the world moving forward onto a sustainable growth path.

The challenges to our institutions are already very visible, but we also need to spell out the implications for attitude and behaviours. Grooming managers and leaders for stardom will be increasingly difficult without an acknowledged ethical code.

The general trend across business now is to focus more on outputs rather than processes. Organisations are increasingly working with consumers to see how they can improve their products and services, and are seeking to forge strategic partnerships with others who can help them develop and deliver what the customer demands. The lines between the public and private sectors are becoming more blurred as a growing number of services are outsourced to contractors in a bid to save costs.

This means that it will become even more important for organisations to be outwardly focused and to be able to exhibit values and ethics that have broad appeal to their range of stakeholders. More companies will need to learn the lessons of the past two years, and exercise constraint and restraint in their public behaviour.

The values and ethics of managers and leaders themselves will need to be increasingly open to scrutiny. Senior pay is just one example of where values and ethics are most publicly displayed, and where there is a growing unease about both rewarding poor performance and pay inequalities. Accounting conventions now require full disclosure of senior pay and rewards. Public sector pay in the UK will also come under the spotlight with the new review body being chaired by Will Hutton.

It has already become apparent that some basic concepts of fairness, equality and justice are being overlooked – partly because they have never been articulated properly.

Because of historic difficulties with pay regulation, it is going to be doubly difficult to regulate pay in the public sector. There are also ongoing issues of low pay and about the affordability of pensions.

In setting top reward strategies, organisations need to make sure they reward and encourage the behaviours that are consistent with the organisational vision and values. The way we value people at the top has never been more important – and avoiding the issue will be impossible.

The following checklist will help organisations put their pay and reward strategy under the spotlight and ensure that it is both appropriate and fair.

 Checklist on senior pay and reward strategy

- Are you aware of the benchmark pay increase for senior managers in your industry/service?
- Does the benchmark pay include a bonus for performance with a percentage of basic pay, or is the bonus genuinely for exceptional performance?
- How is performance assessed?
- At any time in the past ten years, has there ever been an instance in which the bonus has not been paid (in full or in part)?
- Does the organisation have an explicit reward strategy that includes senior pay?
- What constraints are there (e.g. budget limit for pay settlements)?
- What measures are applied to evaluate the behaviour that underpins performance?
- What long-term plan do you have to keep pay and productivity in line with each other?
- Who is accountable for the pay and reward strategy in the organisation and for decisions on senior pay?

Key points

- Values and ethics are integral to managing and leading. However, they need to be clearly expressed, particularly at an organisational level, and there needs to be evaluation and follow-up to see whether values and ethics are being consistently displayed.
- Values and ethics need to be continuously reviewed. Are they fit for purpose? For example, as the impact of recession and government cuts is felt, we must all act responsibly. How is responsibility allocated? Who sets the framework? Organisations need ethical codes – without them, it is difficult to rule on behavioural issues.
- Styles of leadership are changing. Regulation and rule-setting is likely to be less dominant. More engagement and empowerment is needed.
- The direct delivery role of the state is reducing, meaning that the private and voluntary sectors will need to do more.
- Values and ethics are even more important in the public sector, where there is more emphasis on delivering a service and the 'profit line', as such, doesn't exist. The 'Big Society' experiment will be an important part of engaging with values and ethics as a way of improving our communities.
- We need better measures of social cost benefit as we transform public services, and we need better mechanisms for recruiting, developing and evolving volunteers.
- CSR is an important part of business life and has benefits both ways. More and more managers and leaders are looking for ways to make a difference and to develop their skills at the same time.

- Scaling up investment in management and leadership makes sense, even in times of retrenchment. There are lots of cost-effective ways to provide individuals with opportunities to learn and develop, e.g. CPD or ManagementDirect (the CMI learning portal).
- Professional bodies are a great resource for setting standards and codes of ethics, and for creating the right culture within organisations. The standards and codes of ethics are accessible to our members but could also help to underwrite both individual and organisational commitment to good practice.
- Top pay is a big issue that needs to be dealt with rationally and fairly.
- Values and ethics are important from a corporate governance perspective.

In this chapter we have looked at how values and ethics are the bedrock of good management practice. As you have read, in turbulent times a strong set of values can act as a guiding light for managers and leaders who must make difficult decisions. In Chapter 2 we will describe how managers can take a values-driven approach to managing themselves and others.

CHAPTER 2

My question to you is would you want to work for a leader who can't manage or a manager who can't lead? It's not an either/or, it's a both.
Stefan Stern, Director of Strategy, Edelman

A great deal of time, effort and debate has been devoted to separating 'management' from 'leadership'.

I want to reunite the two concepts, which can live very happily together. Leaders need strong and up-to-date management skills, and if they are to be effective in their roles, managers need to understand how to get others to follow them.

In today's flatter, less hierarchical structures, the boundaries of leadership and management are becoming increasingly blurred. Organisations need strong leadership at the helm, but they also need all their managers to take personal responsibility for motivating and empowering their teams.

Being able to manage yourself effectively is an essential prerequisite for leading others. You win the right to lead by role-modelling the behaviour you expect of others. Your competence in the key management disciplines enables you to drive the performance you need from your people.

The business world we now inhabit is moving very fast. Leaders and managers must rise to the challenge of keeping their knowledge and skills up-to-date.

This chapter gives practical guidance on how to effectively manage yourself and how to develop the skills you need to inspire others. It provides some tools and techniques that you can use to assess how well you are doing, as well as examples of how some of today's most influential business leaders approach this task themselves.

Leader insights

Leadership is needed at all levels of the organisation. Everyone is both a manager and a leader to varying degrees at different times. You need both sets of skills.
> Adrian Godfrey, Chair, Institute of Business Consulting and Partner, Ernst & Young

Leadership is about behaviour and management is about competence.
> Terry Morgan, Crossrail

Good managers need to be a bit like a sponge. They absorb issues; distill and contextualise them to try and keep external pressure at a distance from staff focused on delivery.
> Phillippa Williamson, Chief Executive, Serious Fraud Office

Building self-awareness

People who aspire to be responsible for others must first take responsibility for themselves and the way they lead their lives. The role models they create at work, at home and in society, and the degree of satisfaction they take from their business and personal life, have a knock-on effect on those around them. So being an effective leader requires you to put yourself under the microscope and develop better self-knowledge.

For most of us, the annual appraisal is the place where we get feedback about what we are like as managers and how well we are judged to be performing in our jobs. If the appraisal is conducted well, we get a glow of pleasure from a job well done – or we understand more fully why an aspect of the job has gone well or badly.

It's an unfortunate truth, however, that appraisals are not handled well by many organisations. Most of the time they are about past behaviour and the objectives that weren't met, rather than the bigger picture of performance overall and how it can be elevated. In other words, there's a heavy emphasis on what's gone wrong and how we must do better, with scant attention paid to what's gone well and how we can do more of it.

It's interesting that while psychometric and behavioural tools are frequently used as part of the recruitment process, we are much less reflective about what drives good performance once someone is actually in post. When it comes to reviewing performance, these potential sources of intelligence about the individual are often overlooked or bypassed altogether.

If the official appraisal process is lacking, managers need to take matters into their own hands. You need to take stock of your own strengths and weaknesses as an individual, warts and all.

The old adage 'Physician, heal thyself' really does apply to managers, particularly those of us who are constantly seeking to improve our performance. Self-knowledge can come from a number of sources of information, but one of the most effective is peer feedback. This is because it provides rich, in-depth knowledge and reflects the reality of how you are as a manager right now.

Often, a colleague who sees you every day has greater insight than a manager who sees you once a week or month. They see the pressure points on you, the way you manage your work-life balance and how you cope at times of stress. They observe your body language, the courtesy you show to others and the way you conduct yourself in meetings. They know how you react when the spotlight is on you and how well you are able to rise to a challenge.

Many organisations have mechanisms such as 360-degree feedback for regularly giving and receiving this kind of information. But if these formal processes are not in place, there is nothing to stop you actively seeking feedback yourself.

Key points to explore with colleagues are:

- How do I treat you?
- Do you always feel valued and respected?
- Do I take notice of your opinions?

People are often afraid to ask for feedback because they are worried they will not like what they hear. But the data you will get from this kind of frank exchange will tell you what kind of manager you really are.

Be the person you want to be

Managing yourself is not just about understanding your strengths and weaknesses. It is also about challenging and developing yourself to be the person you want to be.

Once you have developed a greater awareness of how you operate, the next step is to try and visualise the kind of manager you want to be. What attributes do you most admire in other managers? Whose style do you particularly relate to? In this respect, you can let your imagination run free.

Most of us will never experience what it is like to work for Richard Branson, Lord Bilimoria, Jamie Oliver or Sir Alex Ferguson, but these may well be our role models. Of course, role models don't have to be well-known business leaders. You may find a role model by looking closer to home – perhaps the best boss you ever had, a memorable teacher, a friend who is a good listener or a business mentor.

Of course this doesn't mean you should try and turn yourself into a carbon copy of someone else. But it is worth reflecting on how the people you admire operate, and thinking about how you might replicate it in a way that feels comfortable and personal to you.

This authenticity in management style is vital. Trying to emulate the brash, no-nonsense, direct approach of someone like Lord Alan Sugar, for example, simply won't work if that's not how you really are. You won't feel comfortable and it will be obvious to other people that you are hiding behind a facade.

The values-led approach we have talked about earlier in Chapter 1 comes into play again here. Managers need a strong sense of their own personal values because it is this value set that dictates the way we go about our jobs.

It's worth spending some time thinking about what your personal values really are and whether you are reflecting these in the way you come across as a manager. Do you value creativity, learning and helping others, for example, or are you driven by risk and financial reward? Is recognition and status important to you, or are you more interested in challenge, innovation and collaboration?

Leader insights

My most influential boss was old-fashioned yet a really unusual character – very inspirational in his own way, and really had a great personal 'touch'. He had no formal qualifications but he could organise, get people to do things, motivate, develop, acknowledge – and all of it without raising his voice.

Steve Holliday, Chief Executive, National Grid

I have been lucky enough to have some great role models, from blunt Northerners to Cabinet Ministers. A peak of my career was serving under David Blunkett, who had the most tremendous ability to think strategically. We would relentlessly focus on adding value, thinking in terms of outcomes rather than processes, and David could relate to people at all levels.

Lord Bichard, founder, Institute for Government

I have learnt more from one or two good leaders, who gave me the opportunity to try things myself, than I did from my MBA.

Phillippa Williamson, Chief Executive, Serious Fraud Office

Developing management skills

To be an effective manager or leader you must also make sure that your basic management competency and skills are up to date. It's tempting to say 'I don't understand the balance sheet so I will employ someone who does', but as you climb higher in the organisation, these basic skills are essential for effective risk and financial management. You will soon find yourself exposed if you don't have them.

Everyone needs a comprehensive grounding in the basics of management if they are to run their department or team successfully. A simple skills analysis will help you identify where your weaknesses lie and plan for how to fill the gaps.

A good starting point is to ask yourself what tasks you find most difficult and in what situations you feel most out of your comfort zone. You can then dig deeper into the specific skills and competencies you need to perform your role and assess how well you match up to them.

It is helpful to involve your line manager in this exercise if possible, so that they can support any necessary development and give feedback on whether your performance has improved as a result. The closing of this feedback loop is often the most important part of all.

Once you've identified the areas where you need to take action, you need to put together a plan on how to fill the gaps. There are numerous options available, ranging from short courses and e-learning programmes to working with a coach or mentor. The formal qualification route is still a popular option, although in these difficult economic times, managers will often have to work hard to make a case for funding by their employer.

If you find yourself in this scenario, it's worth pointing out that the benefit of following a formal course of study is that there is hard evidence of competence at the end. This is valuable for both the individual and the organisation.

How many times have you heard in a recruitment interview that the candidate has ten years' experience as a financial consultant or eight years' experience of managing projects? This tells the organisation the individual has been working in a particular role, but not that they are competent in it. The possession of a relevant qualification helps the organisation ensure there are no gaps in a manager's knowledge and that their skills are up to date.

Leader insight

I like qualifications because they demonstrate personal commitment. Although I work with lots of professionals, very few of them have been adequately prepared for the management and leadership challenges they face.

Phillippa Williamson, Chief Executive, Serious Fraud Office

Managing your time

Managing yourself is also about managing your time: setting clear priorities and keeping them under constant review. The books on this subject are legion, with many different methods.

What most effective time managers have learnt, however, is the importance of distinguishing between the different aspects of their role. There needs to be a balance in the day between thinking time, completing tasks, communicating with people and 'banking' time (the time you allocate to develop knowledge, skills and experience).

It's easy to fall into the trap of just 'completing' tasks – people who do this are not really managing at all. Time just disappears and tomorrow there will be another set of tasks to deal with. A more helpful approach is to set clear goals and objectives for the day/week/month ahead so that you are clear about what you are trying to achieve and how you are going to get there.

The following example illustrates the kind of questions you might need to ask yourself when planning how to effectively manage the time you spend on an important task:

> Imagine you are planning a major reshuffle within your team to accommodate the arrival of a new person who is bringing additional skills and extra capacity.
>
> These questions will help you break the task down into manageable chunks and draw up a schedule of what you need to do and by when.
>
> - What are the tasks I need to complete?
> - Who do I need to involve?
> - Who do I need to communicate with and when?
> - What skills do I need in order to reshuffle the team?
> - Who has the necessary skills and experience to help me?

- What communication strategy have I put in place – from explaining why the reshuffle is being undertaken to communicating difficult decisions?
- How will I manage the potential negative impact/manage risk?
- How will I integrate the new team member?
- How will I judge my success?

In my experience there are three themes that re-occur in every conversation about time management with managers at all levels. They are control, perspective and managing key relationships.

Control

We all have much more control than we think, but we are often too ready to relinquish that control and let others dictate how we manage our time. If you constantly find yourself taking on more work than you can manage, find it difficult to make time to chat with colleagues or constantly have to leave social events early, then you need to get back in control.

A good technique for putting yourself back in the driving seat is to allocate time according to importance rather than urgency. This is easier to say than do, but it is worth making the effort. Many urgent issues cross my desk every week, but there are perhaps only one or two that are also important. So when you are facing conflicting demands, think about whether tasks belong in the 'urgent' or 'important' pile.

Perspective

When you lose control, things quickly get out of perspective. You can start to feel overwhelmed and go into panic mode, chipping little bits off lots of tasks to get people off your back, and not finishing anything properly. At times like this, it helps to step back and spend some time talking about the job and making a plan rather than just blindly doing it. Preserving a sense of humour can also help.

Managing key relationships

It's tempting to put your head down and motor through the job with your door firmly closed and the telephone off the hook. But in the long term, it's important to allocate sufficient time in your day for the people who will guarantee your future success.

Very often we drift out of contact with regular customers, loyal staff and conscientious providers. We need to take time out to spend time with them, or to celebrate their birthdays and the events that are significant to them. We also need to notice their success at work. No employee was ever heard to complain that they received too much acknowledgement or praise at work. Listen to your colleagues, especially when they say they don't have enough access to you. It's too late when they leave.

Relationship management is also fundamental to not wasting time on vexatious issues, trivial disputes and personality clashes – the issues that can dominate every manager's day. These are time stealers that in the long term can have a detrimental impact on health and happiness – allocating time to managing these relationships appropriately can pay off in the end.

Leader insight

Nurturing relationships is at the heart of the manager/leader role. Transactions are not the same thing as relationships. You need to be very good at maintaining contact.
Professor Cary Cooper, Lancaster University Management School

Nurturing relationships is the key task, especially as you move into a leadership position. You have to bring people with you.
Adrian Godfrey, Chair, Institute of Business Consulting and Partner, Ernst & Young

Being a manager meant being able to manage myself. You can't set the right example if you are disorganised and not managing your own environment.

Andrew Summers, Chairman, Steering Board, Companies House

Make time when it is needed. You can't say my door is always open and then not allow people to access you.

Peter Ayliffe, President and Chief Executive, Visa Europe

 Key questions

- Where did my time go today? Was it time well spent? If not, what could I do differently?
- What can I delegate efficiently to others to free up some time for important tasks?
- How do other people think I manage my time?
- How do I maximise each hour of the day and maintain positive motivation at work?
- How do I re-energise myself at 4pm with a busy evening ahead of me?
- How much time do I spend each day on emails? How can I reduce this time by 50%?
- What is the most time-efficient way of tackling this issue? (i.e. in person, by email, on the phone)
- What are the most important tasks I need to complete this week/month?
- Do I routinely get rid of work paper?
- What is my biggest time-waster at work?
- What steps am I taking to reduce time wasted?

Banking time

Banking time is time out for reflection and learning. It's time to digest what is happening to you and those around you (suppliers, customers, employees, colleagues) and thinking about the skills you need to survive and the strengths you need to build.

Very often we analyse tasks without thinking through how we are developing ourselves or others to meet the current challenges. I tend to rely heavily on my management team without reflecting as often as I should on whether they have the skills to do what I require of them. It's even more difficult to do this in relation to oneself.

Banking time can seem like a selfish exercise, but in my opinion it is vital for today's managers and leaders. The manager who is just reacting will not be managing time well. The manager who is thinking 'What have they got to hit me with now?' will probably not roll with the punches and come out stronger – they will eventually buckle under the strain. So build your muscle tone and keep exercising by finding the time every day for a little quiet reflection.

It's also important to build time in for social networking, however busy your working day. Relating to your peers in other industries and organisations can be extremely rewarding both ways.

Some questions to ask when you are reflecting might be:

- What did I learn?
- What do I need to do to handle the situation better?
- What questions should I ask my colleagues?
- How can I become more proficient in the areas where I lack confidence or competence?
- How do I put a smile on X's face?
- Whose opinions matter most to me in this organisation?
- What techniques have I used to keep my mind/body fresh at work?
- How many times today did I say yes when the answer was probably a no?

Leader insight

Looking back, I would have been more curious and spent longer debating alternative courses of action. Setting a clear focus for yourself and the organisation is critically important – but so is listening and reflecting on experience.

Jonathan Perks, Global CEO Leadership Coach

Leading others

Concepts and theories about leadership abound. A simple Google search will turn up numerous books and academic articles about the competencies, qualities and characteristics required by those who find themselves at the helm of organisations.

As we have seen earlier in this chapter, a lot of the personal qualities required to lead others successfully come from self-knowledge. Many of the leaders interviewed for this book also described how they were driven by an early ambition to lead.

'I made a conscious decision to be a leader when I was 17 and joined the Duke of Edinburgh's Award scheme, but I think my mindset was always about making something of my life,' said former Penna MD and global CEO leadership coach Jonathan Perks.

'I always wanted to be a leader. I was MD by 33 and the groundwork was laid at university where I learnt a lot from organising clubs, events and activities,' says Andrew Summers, Chair of the CMI's Board of Companions.

It's probably fair to say that some people are 'born' leaders. They seem to have an innate ability to instil confidence, command respect and inspire others. These qualities don't come naturally to everyone, but with hard work and determination it is possible to develop them.

As Peter Ayliffe, President and CEO of VisaEurope, says: 'Leadership is about inspiration *and* perspiration'.

The key qualities of a good leader – clarity of vision, high emotional intelligence, top-notch communication skills – haven't changed. But the context in which leaders have to apply these skills has altered almost beyond recognition.

The challenge for future leaders is to keep pace with the dramatic changes taking place in the world of work, and to respond in the way they look ahead, plan and engage with the people they need to follow them.

In his book *Inspiring Leadership*, renowned leadership coach Jonathan Perks suggests that business leaders can learn from the military world in order to become truly inspirational in these chaotic times. Perks, who previously served in the British Army, argues that grey times produce grey leaders – whereas what is really needed is for business leaders to stand up, inspire others and be counted.

Based on his military and international business experience, Perks outlines a blueprint for success based on an eight-point compass model. The eight principal components that make up the model and embody an inspiring leader are:

1   IQ – cognitive intelligence and wisdom
2   Presence – personal power
3   EQ – emotional and social intelligence
4   Appreciation – of others and self
5   MQ – moral intelligence, values and beliefs
6   Passion – love and inspiration
7   SQ – spiritual intelligence, meaning and purpose
8   Service – serve to lead.

Perks suggests that leaders who adopt these eight principles will become more successful, happier and able to live their lives 'on purpose'. (Copies of *Inspiring Leadership* are available from www.jonathanperks.com.)

Leader insight

I always wanted to be a leader. I was inspired by my father, a senior officer in the Indian Army, although he was somewhat disappointed to find that I wanted to make beer.

Lord Bilimoria, Chairman, Cobra Beer Partnership

Work – but not as we know it

The way work is organised has changed fundamentally in recent years: markets have become more sophisticated and truly multinational; technology has speeded up the design and production of goods and services; and the Internet has revolutionised the way we communicate with customers and organise day-to-day business transactions.

The gap between large and small businesses has also narrowed considerably. Although some markets are still dominated by large players who rely on economies of scale, many others have been thrown wide open. Small businesses can now trade all over the world using the Internet to gain market knowledge and reach out to consumers.

This had led to dramatic changes in the way we approach and organise work itself. Organisational hierarchies have become flatter, with more emphasis on smaller, specialised units populated by highly valued 'knowledge' workers. Talent is at a premium – even in times of economic difficulty – with job mobility on the increase and organisations having to work ever harder to retain high-performing and high-potential employees.

The climate in which we operate has also changed. We now do business 24/7 and, thanks to advances in technology, are able to connect with customers and colleagues anytime and from anywhere.

All this has far-reaching implications for the way that organisations need to lead and manage their teams. Managers have to give their teams more independence, authority and responsibility than ever before – and must trust them to use it wisely. Those in senior positions also need to plan differently, adapt to change more rapidly and become more flexible in their approach.

Planning ahead

There has been a sharp shift away from long-term plans towards broad, aspirational visions, coupled with short-term planning. We do, of course, still need to have a focus on the future, but any plans that work too far ahead are almost certainly not worth the paper they are written on. They will soon be outdated by business circumstances, changes in personnel and technological advances. It is important to recognise, however, that if values are intrinsic to the goals a business sets, the chances of these plans or goals experiencing longevity are greater.

Managing change

Leaders need to expand their capability to manage change and take employees on the journey with them. The most effective leaders are often restless individuals who are always looking for scope for improvement and challenging 'the way things are done around here'. Leaders also need to help their teams cope with the uncertainty that is now a factor of everyday business life. We talk more about this in Chapter 3.

Developing the 'F' factor

Leaders need to get better at 'flexing' their managerial muscles. They need a rounded perspective, as well as the ability to take the views of others on board and respond appropriately. Successful leaders take the view that if markets are changing, then the habits of those who serve them must change too. We have to learn to be more flexible and adaptable, or our products and services will quickly become outdated.

Engaging employees

The recent government-commissioned McLeod report, *Engaging for Success: Enhancing Performance through Employee Engagement,* identified employee engagement as one of the biggest and most critical challenges facing organisations today. Leaders need to develop a much better understanding of what the workforce wants, what motivates employees and what they need to do to tap into that all-important 'discretionary effort' that makes the difference between good and outstanding performance.

Leaders who want to improve their ability to inspire and motivate people need to look closely at how they are approaching the following challenges.

Adapting your leadership style

Much has been written over the years about leadership styles, but some of the latest thinking suggests that it's not a question of which style is right or wrong – more a case of choosing the style that's right for the circumstances.

Warwick Business School's Jean Hartley says that leaders need to gain a deeper understanding of the different styles of leadership and the situations where they can be used to best effect. In a recent edition of the CMI's magazine *Professional Manager,* she describes three types of problem or challenge that might arise in a health service setting and outlines the different styles of leadership required to tackle them.

First there are 'tame' problems – issues that are likely to have arisen before and for which known solutions already exist. Everyone knows what needs to be done; the challenge is to actually make it happen. One example of a tame problem in the health service would be the need to wash hands to prevent the spread of infection in hospitals. This type of problem is best dealt with through technical leadership, where the manager's role is to provide the resources, people and processes needed to solve the problem.

A 'wicked' problem, on the other hand, is one where there is no agreed solution, people may see the issue differently and there is a large degree of uncertainty. An example of this in an NHS setting might be how to tackle the health issues related to childhood obesity. This calls for a more 'adaptive' style of leadership, where the manager's role is to ask the right questions and orchestrate the work of a range of people to try and help solve the problem.

Finally there are 'critical' problems where immediate and urgent action is needed, such as dealing with the aftermath of a major road traffic accident in the A&E department. This is one of the occasions when a 'command and control' style of leadership becomes more appropriate.

'Too many organisations have tried to develop a leadership model that says you have to have these qualities or you have to behave in this way. What we are saying is, start off by thinking what is the problem or challenge you are trying to deal with, and then consider what kind of leadership is going to be most appropriate and effective,' she says (*Leadership for Healthcare*, Jean Hartley and John Benington, The Policy Press, 2010).

Leader insights

The future belongs to those who focus on what they contribute, not on what they can take. If you bring value to the table, rewards will come.
Adrian Godfrey, Chair, Institute of Business Consulting and Partner, Ernst & Young

Good managers facilitate. They are assertive only when necessary and see themselves as enablers.
Nigel Meager, Director, Institute for Employment Studies (IES)

Leadership is more about strategy – conceptualising the future, setting broad aims and communicating the vision. Management is more about the actual grind of implementation, charting progress and keeping a hand on the tiller. People in senior positions must do both, seeing the wood and the trees.

Sir Paul Judge, Chairman, Schroder Income Growth Fund

Leaders create the environment in which things happen. They step back rather than hold on.

Jackie Orme, Chief Executive, Chartered Institute of Personnel and Development (CIPD)

Setting standards

In a challenging economic environment, there is often a tendency to focus on targets. Organisations need employees to deliver the results that will ensure not just success over the competition, but often survival. The result is that they set ever higher and more stretching targets in a bid to motivate employees to achieve corporate goals.

There are, of course, many situations where targets are appropriate, but I would argue that future leaders need to be more proactive in setting standards. It's important to recognise the difference between the two. When people are working to a target, they will often do the minimum necessary to achieve it. The language and appeal of standards is very different. A standard requires the individual to achieve work of a certain quality, rather than just hitting the right number.

Take the example of the UK charity the National Society for the Prevention of Cruelty to Children (NSPCC), where in the mid-1990s new standards of child protection were set for social workers. The focus shifted away from the number of cases taken on towards satisfactory outcomes in terms of families reunited and improved access to services for some of the most vulnerable people in society.

Social workers were encouraged to aspire towards standards that actually impacted directly on children and family welfare. They were trained and developed to achieve these standards rather than being measured on how many visits they had conducted.

By contrast, you only have to look at the public sector to see the negative impact that can result from too heavy an emphasis on targets. Reform programmes in the public sector often fail because targets are imposed from above in response to some strategic or political imperative. These targets often bear little relation to the reality of life on the front line, but managers are nevertheless expected to achieve them. Scant attention is paid to issues such as ownership, commitment and the actual capability of the team to deliver what is being asked of them. As a result, the project flounders and the blame is laid at the door of managers, who are perceived to have 'failed' to deliver.

Leaders and managers who work in this kind of challenging, target-driven environment need to try and take more control of the target-setting process. The challenge is to interpret what our 'masters' say they want into outcomes that can actually be delivered and have some meaning for customers and stakeholders.

This approach calls for sensitivity, flexibility and the ability to understand the concerns of parties on both sides of the equation. Political nous is needed to communicate effectively upwards about what can realistically be achieved. A strategic approach to communication has to be adopted to ensure employees understand what is needed, know what resources are at their disposal and are engaged with the project to the point where they have the drive and determination to succeed.

Leader insights

When you manage other people you need to create an environment where they can get on with it. Setting standards and expectations is the key factor, not micro-managing. Advice, direction, help and encouragement work much better than command and control.

Rita Clifton, UK Chairman, Interbrand

The biggest learning curve in management is learning when to let go and knowing how to create an environment where other people can perform.

David Noble, Chief Executive, Chartered Institute of Purchasing and Supply (CIPS)

Managing boundaries

Boundaries come in many guises in organisations. Some are practical while others are political. Some are necessary for safety and compliance while others appear to have become established for no good reason. Some boundaries are overt and explicit, while others may be hidden and unspoken.

Managing these boundaries and helping employees successfully negotiate their way around them is a key task for managers and leaders in today's organisations.

Setting boundaries is particularly important at times of change and uncertainty. Restructuring and re-engineering programmes, for example, often get derailed because the managers at the heart of the change are not quite sure what authority they have. It's important to recognise that telling people they are important is not the same as empowering them. The leader's role is to make sure people are clear about the vision, how it will be achieved and what they personally have permission to do in pursuit of the end goal.

Breaking down unnecessary boundaries is equally important. The barriers that often spring up in organisations between functions and departments are an obvious example. If people are allowed to become defensive and protective of their own patch, they will end up working in silos. Managers and leaders need to convey a strong message that it is collaboration, not competition, that will produce the best results.

Uncovering hidden boundaries that are hampering progress within a business is another key task. One of the most common hidden boundaries is around the recruitment and development of talent. We are less likely these days to see flagrant discrimination, but that does not mean that organisations yet fully understand how to value or promote diversity in their teams. (We talk more about managing diversity in Chapter 9.)

Managers often seem unable to look beyond the type of person who has traditionally filled a particular role and are stuck in a rut of recruiting for skills alone. Forward-looking organisations, however, are beginning to realise that recruiting for potential and developing for skills gives them access to a much wider pool of talent. The end result will be a more flexible workforce that is equipped with the diverse range of skills necessary for success in today's fast-moving competitive environment.

Leader insight

People worry a lot about giving people too much scope. In my experience this is not a real danger as most people operate miles inside the boundaries. When you ask them what's constraining them, they often have no answer.

Steve Holliday, Chief Executive, National Grid

Taking responsibility for failure

Managers and leaders who find themselves at the sharp end of delivery must also be prepared to take responsibility for failure. It's not good enough to blame the system or someone else in the system. Those who can't or won't be held accountable for the results or behaviour of their team are failing to set appropriate standards and can't expect others to follow them and act appropriately.

Managers must ensure that they are not setting themselves up for failure by being prepared to challenge inappropriate behaviour in others. This might come in the shape of poor performance, bullying, aggression towards suppliers or customers, dishonesty, or a casual attitude to deadlines. All of these behaviours reflect on the manager and need to be identified and tackled at an early stage.

Unless this doctrine of accountability is heard, understood and consistently implemented, the organisation will not hang together as it should and employees will lack the motivation to perform at their peak.

Leader insight

When you have doubts about someone it is almost always right to act quickly rather than slowly. We sometimes allow situations which we know won't get better to carry on.

Sir John Sunderland, former Non-executive Chairman,
Cadbury Schweppes

Celebrating success

Is your organisation's cup half full or half empty? It's a sad fact that in business we tend to focus more on what's gone wrong than on what's gone right. A positive approach that embraces celebration of success enables both individuals and organisations to feel good about themselves. As a result of this feel-good factor, those organisations will be better to work for, more pleasant and rewarding to deal with – and their success should breed further success.

Anyone who has worked for an employer where there were no opportunities to celebrate success will have experienced feeling rejected and excluded. Employees who have gone the extra mile to pursue a team or departmental goal are unlikely to do so again if there is no reward or recognition for their efforts.

Managers and leaders need to think carefully about the behaviours they want to recognise and reward, and put mechanisms in place to do so. It's not just the big successes that count. Recognising the achievements of small milestones along the way to a bigger goal can be extremely motivating and will encourage people to keep going.

External industry or business awards can also be very motivating. The 500-plus companies that enter the UK's National Business Awards every year have clearly recognised the value of promoting excellent practice from within their teams. As a serial attendee and judge at many awards ceremonies over the years, I can tell you that recognition makes a tangible difference and is entirely disproportionate to the money invested.

Leader insight

Delivery and completion are very important and always need to be recognised and rewarded.

Helen Brand, CEO, Association of Chartered Certified Accountants (ACCA)

Valuing and developing your people

The phrase 'people are our most important asset' has become a corporate mantra, but how many organisations actually measure their leadership and management capability, and the impact it has on the bottom line?

In today's knowledge-intensive economy, as much as 80% of a company's worth is tied to human capital. It's unfortunate, therefore, that we do not yet have a consistent and meaningful way of measuring this 'intangible' asset.

Today, more than ever, we need accurate data to help us understand the people side of the business and the return we get from investing in skills and development.

The CMI is currently working with Business in the Community (BITC) and other professional bodies to try and develop a framework for measurement of human capital.

This framework will help managers to take a proactive approach to current management practices that are successful and to benchmark themselves against best practice.

Managers also need to look at the systems they have in place for identifying and developing high-potential employees and at whether the culture encourages people to develop their skills with a view to moving into more stretching roles. The CIPD (www.cipd.co.uk) has information and resources which can help to guide managers through this task.

Leader insights

Wherever you look, your job as a manager is to make your people be the best they can be – and usually they don't know just how good they could be. It's individuals that make the difference.

Sir Alan Jones, Chairman Emeritus, Toyota UK, quoted in the McLeod Report on employee engagement

Management development and training is taken seriously at ACAS. We don't expect people to function on empty.

Ed Sweeney, Chair, ACAS

A good boss recognises when the other person has a different skill set and seeks to draw out these strengths.

Terry Morgan, Chairman, Crossrail

I tend not to talk to people about their future as a manager or leader. I observe them and support and encourage. I give them some extra responsibility and watch how they manage themselves and the situation. I involve them in management discussions and assess the results. You always know when someone has reached their natural level.

Sir David Howard, Chairman, Charles Stanley

Communicating with purpose

In a world where managers and leaders are universally mistrusted, it can be tempting to give up on communication. When times are tough, however, quitting is not an option.

Research has shown that communicating clearly with people is even more important when it comes to delivery. If employees know what is going on in the organisation and feel a part of it, there is a corresponding impact on performance – and ultimately on profit.

The key to successful communication is today's turbulent business environment is to constantly adapt, change and innovate in the way we communicate. Managers and leaders need to get better at exploiting formal communication channels within organisations, but they also have to learn how to tap into the informal communication that happens outside of their control – in the staff restaurant, around the water cooler or on social networking sites – and that can be really effective in bringing about dialogue opportunities.

Too often in organisations, formal communication is one-way. There is no opportunity for views to be exchanged, for new ideas to be contributed or for managers to check that messages have been received and understood.

The biggest barrier to transforming corporate communication into a two-way street is fear. Managers worry about how they will cope if people reject or resist the message. They are afraid of opening their intranets up for debate or encouraging active use of networks such as LinkedIn or Facebook in case inappropriate content is published or sensitive corporate information leaks out.

It's important for managers to recognise that if people are negative about the communication they put out, they are sometimes giving feedback about the message (they don't like it) and sometimes about the method chosen. Managers need to learn to distinguish between the two.

Many organisations have also learnt the hard way that if they don't give employees access to communication channels, they will simply 'go underground' and have the conversations outside the business instead. Witness the company that banned the use of social networking sites, only to find that 2000 of its employees had signed up to an unofficial Facebook group.

The truth is that if people are given the freedom to communicate they will reward the organisation with feedback and ideas that it would otherwise never have access to. A good example of how this works in practice is government green papers, which allow third parties to comment on both the policy itself and the implementation issues. The final proposals – for changes to employment law, for example – are often significantly altered and enhanced as a result of the contributions made at the consultation stage.

The key to success is to choose the communication tool that's fit for purpose – never communicate a redundancy decision via email, for example. If there is a complex message to deliver, think carefully about whether the best way to do that might be face-to-face.

The most important issue for managers, however, is to make sure that they are clear about the real purpose of any significant piece of communication. The reality is that most of the communication that senior business leaders do is with a view to getting others to buy into their ideas. They are not purely communicating, they are selling – whether that's an ambition, an objective, the benefits of a business decision or the reason behind a product or service development.

Leaders and managers have to sell the message – but they also have to sell themselves as the visible, lead person who is taking responsibility for a particular set of actions or decisions.

Key questions

- Does your approach to leadership reflect the new world of work?
- Do you have a toolkit of leadership skills you can call on to suit different circumstances?
- Have you set clear standards for your team to work to?
- What boundaries – overt or hidden – exist in your organisation? What can you do to manage them more successfully?
- Are you role-modelling the behaviours you would like to see in your team, particularly with regard to taking accountability for actions?
- What mechanisms can you put in place to celebrate your team's achievements and successes?
- Are you giving sufficient priority to developing management capability in your team?
- What steps can you take to improve your communication competence?
- Are you making full use of the internet as a communication medium? For example, through Twitter you can reach a whole professional network in three seconds and analyse its response. Twitter, unlike surveys, is free, and provides real up-to-the-minute information.

In this chapter we have looked at some of the practical tools and techniques managers can employ to help them develop personally and at how they can develop styles and approaches that will inspire others. In Chapter 3, we go on to look at the specific skills that managers need to cope with the constant turbulence of today's business environment and to successfully drive through change.

CHAPTER 3

All managers must be able to deal with ambiguity – comfortable straight lines don't work any more.
Stephen Howard, Chief Executive, Business in the Community

In today's turbulent business environment, the only certainty is uncertainty. The very speed of organisational change sometimes leaves managers gasping for breath.

Technological innovations, changing consumer preferences and a challenging economic environment mean that no business can remain static for very long. This is good news in one way. We are part of a dynamic economy in which there will always be opportunity for growth, unsatisfied demand and a number of potential sources of competitive advantage.

The ambiguity and uncertainty that run alongside this constant upheaval, however, pose enormous challenges for those at the helm of organisations. Wherever you look in the public or private sector, you see leaders and managers trying to balance the books and compete for business while anticipating the next wave of change.

The old certainties just don't exist anymore. Witness the recent credit crisis, which caused seismic shockwaves across the world as it became clear that the financial institutions previously perceived as 'safe' were in danger of coming tumbling down. The fact that major banks could have collapsed without government intervention on an unprecedented scale has shaken the very foundations of everything we believed about our economy and the way business is conducted.

There is now a huge amount of debt in the system, and the only way to redress this is to cut costs and increase productivity, both in the public and private sector. This means we rely increasingly on the skills and experience of managers and leaders to make optimal decisions about financial risk while at the same time investing in growth.

Do those currently at senior level in our organisations have the skills to manage in this new reality? The evidence suggests that there is still a huge gap in our ability to lead major change initiatives successfully. Research has shown that many, if not most, change programmes fail to some extent – often because organisations simply don't have the ability to move quickly and flex their services to meet new and emerging customer requirements.

This is not a situation we can allow to continue. UK plc needs to invest urgently in raising management and leadership skill levels so that we can raise our game and achieve sustainable competitive advantage.

This chapter looks at what managers and leaders have to do to respond more effectively to their changing environment. It also outlines some of the practical steps that individuals can take to improve their day-to-day management of change and uncertainty, and provides examples of best practice.

Leader insights

Managers process things but leaders change them.
David Noble, Chief Executive, Chartered Institute of Purchasing and Supply (CIPS)

For young people entering a management career, I always say they must expect to be change managers. Effective implementation requires managers to be comfortable with ambiguity and their commitment as individuals, and as part of a team, to make things happen despite the many barriers that will be put in their way.

Charles Tilley, Chief Executive, Chartered Institute
of Management Accountants (CIMA)

Planning for change

It's all too easy to feel overwhelmed when you're under pressure to cut budgets and make radical changes. It's important to recognise, however, that change often presents a valuable opportunity to refocus and think about what the real priorities are.

In periods of stability, organisations often experience vision and mission 'creep'. They start to deliver new activities with little evidence of demand that, in turn, provide little return on investment.

When you find yourself compelled to make sweeping changes, it is often a good idea to go back to basics and define the core activities for the business or your particular department or team.

The following step-by-step approach breaks the task of refocusing down into manageable chunks and will help you create a clear picture of what the future direction of travel should be.

Step 1
First, you need to develop a clear understanding of the cost base of your organisation.

- If staff are your biggest expenditure and asset, you need to assess the amount you are spending in your staffing budget and work out if the balance of the workforce is right. Typically, when trade is down you need to spend more on product sales and marketing.

- A zero-based approach to budgeting is also helpful at this stage. So question each area of spend and start to build from there. How could you reduce your staff or other overheads, for example? Do you have any internal functions that could be run more efficiently? What opportunities are there to streamline administration?
- Make economies wherever you can and don't delay taking action. Organisations with flatter structures, streamlined administration and efficient sales operations will do better when times are tough.

Step 2

Second, look at all your income generators:

- Which products or services have been relatively unaffected by recession and which are still growing?
- What are your biggest earners? Which activities take up time and resources but produce the least profit?
- How can you redouble your commitment to the most profitable areas, so that you can generate enough cash reserves to keep your operation afloat? If you take a cross-functional approach you will find greater savings and more revenues than if you look at individual income streams and cost centres.

Step 3

Third, do some environmental scanning and competitor analysis. Key questions to ask are:

- How is the market managing?
- Who are the winners or losers? Is their success/failure likely to continue?

- How does it affect the USP of the company we are in? (Take the example of the Chartered Management Institute [CMI]. There are lots of providers of management and leadership training, but we are the only chartered body and this is a position we need to further exploit. At the same time, we may be able to reap economies of scale from cooperation with other chartered bodies).

Refocusing in this way helps to ensure that people in the business are spending their time profitably. It also reduces some of the time-pressured stress that people feel as a result of additional risk and uncertainty.

Once you are clear about the way ahead, you need to plan for change in the way you would for any major project. Your plan of action should cover:

- **Vision:** What is the 'big idea' behind the change? What is the organisation striving to achieve? This must be clear and compelling.
- **Scope:** What needs to change if the organisation is to realise its vision?
- **Time frame:** What will change, when, and in what order? Radical change takes time, especially if attitude change is involved.
- **People:** Who will be most affected by change and how? Who are the 'change agents' that will play a prominent role in making change happen on the ground?
- **Resources:** How much will the change cost? Will there be offsetting benefits?
- **Communications:** Will you need new mechanisms and structures to communicate with front-line employees?
- **Training:** Have you budgeted for training managers and front-line employees in both the hard and soft skills associated with change?
- **Organisation structure:** Will changes to the structure be needed? Will the business need to move towards a flatter structure, for example?

Leader insights

One thing that is for sure is that the plan you have just written will need lots of amendments and flexibility. You need to be communicating risks and opportunities all the time. You need to ask simple questions such as if I invest in this and the market doesn't grow, what do I do? Am I over-reliant on one or two products or services? If I do a joint venture and it doesn't work out, what is my exit strategy?

Paul Idzik, Chief Executive, DTZ Holdings plc

Knowledge is adding to your capability every day – wisdom is letting go of something every day.

Lord Bilimoria, Chairman, Cobra Beer Partnership

Managing in an upturn is about maximising volume growth. In a downturn, it's about value, innovation and doing more with less. The disciplines are different.

Calvert Markham, Managing Director, Elevation Learning

Building the right culture

Change will only truly happen when the concept is fully embraced by everyone involved. Ambiguity and uncertainty are extremely unsettling for employees and any change programme will inevitably be met by a degree of scepticism or resistance.

There is much groundwork, however, that managers can do to create a more accepting culture where employees feel safe to raise their concerns and engage in the process of change.

You can develop a culture that supports change by:

- Recognising prevalent value systems
- Creating a blame-free culture of empowerment and pushing down decision-making – while also clarifying decision boundaries
- Breaking down departmental barriers
- Designing challenging jobs
- Freeing time for risk and innovation
- Focusing on the interests of all stakeholders.

It can be useful to appoint a 'champion' for change, i.e. a lead person who will be able to galvanise the troops into action. Their credibility will be of paramount importance, as will sufficient seniority and a proven track record. A change leader should be lively, energetic, passionate and committed. If you are not the right person to be leading the change, you need to recognise it at the start and seek the right support.

In organisations you need champions from every part of the business. For example, at the National Society for the Prevention of Cruelty to Children (NSPCC), we appointed change champions at a relatively junior level because they were the most influential in terms of changing practices on the front line.

It's also important to build a change team with a mix of technical competencies, personal styles and levels of seniority – ideally, respected individuals from within the organisation. You need 'movers and shakers' whose commitment is not in doubt, although it can be a good idea to temper the mix with a few known cynics.

These individuals will be instrumental in helping to build employee engagement and commitment, and in creating a culture where your change programme can progress and flourish.

Leader insights

Never by-pass your managers or risk letting them feel undermined. If you build trust with them, they will go the extra mile.

Martin Bean, Vice Chancellor, The Open University

Making the case for change is not the same as taking things forward.

David Noble, Chief Executive, Chartered Institute of Purchasing and Supply (CIPS)

Developing a communication strategy

It's essential to have a sound communication strategy and to create a dialogue around change. If people don't buy in, or feel disregarded, this can seriously undermine the whole change process.

You need to make sure that employees at every level of the organisation understand the reasons for change and know what will be happening, when it will be happening and what is expected of them. Don't assume that everything is clear to everyone after a single message – communication should be ongoing. Give regular updates and progress reports, making sure to report on early wins and celebrate successes. Provide opportunities for employees to input their ideas and seek clarification where necessary.

Be open and honest with employees about the likely extent of change. Don't allow rumours to circulate – be frank. If you can't answer, say you don't know and give an indication of when you might be able to say more.

Make sure you also communicate with external stakeholders such as customers and suppliers, for example. They will be able to provide valuable views and insights to help you shape your ideas, and it's vital to also keep them on side and up to date with any changes on the horizon.

You might want to consider using social media as a tool to engage employees and other interested parties. It's an excellent way of getting just-in-time feedback and taking the temperature of how people are feeling. It's important to recognise that if you don't give people free access to these mechanisms internally, they will go outside the business and find unofficial channels in which to voice their views and concerns.

Leader insight

It is not only a good thing to take people with you, it is essential if you want to be successful in the medium and long term. Your senior team will help you manage change if they buy into, own and run the necessary changes.

Martin Bean, Vice Chancellor, The Open University

Building employee commitment

The best way to get people on board and actively supporting change is to involve them in the process. This means that a key role for managers leading change is to build relationships with employees, develop an in-depth understanding of how their teams work and to recognise both the limitations and strengths of these teams.

People need a clear understanding of the reasons for change before they will fully buy into it. You need to explain the business case for change and paint a picture of what the organisation will look like when the change programme has been implemented. How will the structure change? What impact will there be on roles and responsibilities? What will the new culture feel like? What kind of behaviours will be recognised and rewarded in the new scenario?

It's important to make this a two-way dialogue and to give people the opportunity to ask questions, contribute ideas and generally make their voice heard. It can sometimes be helpful to get employees to identify the change factors for themselves via workshops, focus groups or team meetings. This will help them see and understand the need for change and will create a sense of 'ownership' of the process.

It's also helpful wherever possible to personalise the case for change, which people are more likely to accept if they can relate to their own job and team. An important role for line managers is to translate the corporate case for change into something that every individual in the company can relate to. This means considering what change will mean for each individual in terms of status (job title, budget responsibility); habits (changes to working time, new colleagues); beliefs (i.e., move to a customer focus); and behaviour (new working practices).

You can build commitment by:

- Sharing information as widely as possible
- Allowing for suggestions and input, and encouraging widespread participation
- Breaking changes into manageable chunks and minimising surprises
- Making standards and requirements clear
- Being honest about the downside.

Leader insight

Taking people with you on a journey is very important to managing change. They need to understand the direction of travel and the pitstops. They also need to know you will help if needed.

Stefan Stern, Director of Strategy, Edelman

Case study: Overcoming barriers to change

Corus Strip Products UK (CSP UK) is based at Port Talbot and Llanwern, Newport in South Wales. CSP UK makes steel in strip form. This is used in markets such as vehicle manufacture, construction, electrical appliances, tubes and packaging.

The business has been through an ongoing change programme – known as The Journey – both in the lead-up to and since becoming part of the Indian-owned Tata group.

The company wanted to address a wide range of business challenges, but the common theme was the fundamental way that people at all levels went about their work. A set of eight core values was developed, in consultation with employees and wider stakeholders, to provide the guiding principles by which Corus people would work.

The following case study excerpt, taken from *The Times Top 100 Business Case Studies* edition 15, demonstrates how the business approached the task of overcoming barriers to change.

Change may challenge people's abilities, experience, customs and practice. It may even be seen as a threat. This can create resistance or barriers to change. For example, if job roles are changed, employees and managers may feel that they lose status or power. If jobs are cut, remaining employees may feel insecure. This can cause low morale and lead to poor productivity.

Although Corus Steel Strip Products as a company supported the principles of change and innovation, not all previous programmes had delivered the required results.

Corus is an established business in a traditional industry. This meant that it had set patterns of doing things in some areas of the business. This attitude of 'this is the way we do things around here' made it more difficult to make necessary changes. Some Corus employees had a fear of the unknown and saw new initiatives as a possible threat to their existing teams and positions. Job reductions had been a major theme in the steel industry since the 1970s and some of Corus' previous change initiatives had led to job cuts. Other people did not see a threat to their job because the business had previously survived difficult times. This complacency made change difficult for Corus.

Another issue facing Corus was its ageing workforce. There is a considerable degree of expertise in the company and long-term high rewards kept people within the industry. Older employees with high technical skills stayed because these skills were not easily transferable. Fewer young people were attracted to the industry because of reduced job opportunities and reductions in apprenticeship schemes across the UK.

The company also had a history of rewarding 'long service' rather than 'distinguished service'. This means that employees who had been with the company a long time (but who had lower productivity) could be gaining greater rewards than newer employees who were producing more. Corus felt this was an area that needed major change so that those employees with higher output were suitably rewarded.

Overcoming barriers

'We cannot solve our problems by spending; we cannot solve our problems by cutting back. The only way to meet our challenges is to change how we go about things ...' (quote from the Managing Director of CSP UK)

One of the key techniques Corus has used to overcome resistance to change has been to work closely with employees and get them involved as much as possible in the programme. From the start it was important for the company to share with employees what might happen to the business if it didn't change. Corus put emphasis on getting everyone to take ownership of the new values by physically signing up to the programme. This helped them to 'buy into' the new ways of working. Workers are now more involved in decision making and their contributions and experience are recognised. Through a range of direct and indirect communications, for example, weekly newsletters and workshops, Corus ensures that all employees understand what behaviours it expects of them.

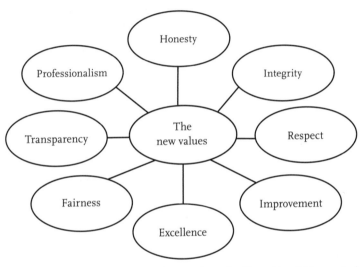

Figure 3.1 The 'new values' diagram from the *Times Top 100* case study

As part of implementation, Corus needed to highlight how people were behaving. It created a programme with 'shock tactics' to show managers and employees the condition of the plant, to identify weaknesses and encourage employees to make changes. For example, 150 senior managers were invited to the Millennium Stadium in Cardiff. This impressive venue raised expectations. However, they were served cold tea and given a presentation on a ripped projector screen.

The fact that attendees did not comment on this demonstrated that people did not see they had a 'right to challenge'. It also highlighted that employees had become accustomed to working with limited resources and were willing to accept low standards. This would be an important aspect to work on during the culture change. Managers were also shown videos of poor working conditions and interviews with local schoolchildren in which they said they would not work at the plant because of their perception of a poor outlook and a poor working environment.

Around 150 workshops were held to spread the messages. Fortnightly newspapers clarified these values and repeated the key messages through articles on various activities, such as employees taking part in the redesign of a control room to improve layout and safety. Billboards, intranet, video programmes and most of all, direct one-to-one conversations all reinforced the message.

The Journey change programme at Corus Strip Products contributes to sustainability for the business. By facing up to its internal weaknesses, the company has improved efficiency, increased output, lowered costs and reduced waste in an increasingly competitive steel market. This has enabled the business not just to survive but to grow – even during the economic recession of 2008 and 2009.

(Copyright *The Times 100* and MBA Publishing Ltd, www.thetimes100.co.uk.)

Since the time of writing, Corus has changed its name to Tata Steel Strip Products UK.

Dealing with the politics

Managing change means taking on the politics within the organisation. Every organisation will have its change 'saboteurs', those who will consciously or unconsciously act in ways that impede progress. The challenge for managers is to identify what and who may be blocking progress and to find ways of breaking through the barriers.

There is quite often no particular malicious intent. Sometimes people have a vested interest in maintaining the status quo because a planned change will result in a loss of power or status. Often people resist change because of fear. No one has taken the trouble to explain the planned changes to them properly and, as a result, they are anxious about what it might mean for them.

Once you've identified the driving and restraining forces, you need to plan to reinforce the drivers and weaken or lessen the forces that are holding change back. Once again, this calls for open, honest and regular communication.

Be prepared for conflict and try and bring it to the surface rather than allow it to fester. Conflict can often be put to positive use, especially if you tackle it by examining and analysing it with those who are experiencing it. For example, open discussion and clarification can lead to the resolution of difficulties and the introduction of improvements.

If conflict cannot be resolved through improved explanation and discussion, you will have to negotiate and persuade. This means avoiding getting into any entrenched positions yourself, and working out how to shift others if they dig their heels in too deeply. It means getting to an agreed 'yes' without either side winning or losing face. You can't bulldoze through resistance to change – you need to listen and persuade. This will usually be a slow process, but it can be helped by frank discussion and even more by positive success. Help and guidance in managing the politics in organisations is available via a diagnostic toolkit 'Leading with political awareness' developed by the CMI with

Warwick Business School, Atkins and the Improvement & Development Agency. (See Resources section.)

Leader insights

I have had to deal with complexity, ambiguity and politics in local and central government. This gives you valuable insights into how other people see the world and improves your ability to navigate.

Lord Bichard, founder, Institute for Government

You need to be able to challenge unhelpful behaviours without taking away individuality.

John Taylor, Chief Executive, ACAS

Equipping people to manage change

If people are to manage change successfully, they need the skills, competencies and resources to do it. Change that is poorly implemented can be very damaging for the 'survivors', and organisations have a responsibility to equip their managers appropriately.

As we have seen earlier in this chapter, good people management and communication skills are essential, but project management and the ability to manage resources effectively are also important. Managers who are both confident and competent in this critical area will be better able to drive the change programmes that they have been charged with.

A good approach is to view the change programme as a learning process itself and to integrate it into the corporate training programme. This will enable you to build both technical and soft skills at all levels of the organisation as the change programme unfolds.

If you can turn learning into something that people want to 'buy into' and can apply straight away back on the front line, then so much the better. The buzz of 'discovery' that they experience will help to build commitment and engagement as they begin to see the results of their learning in action.

> **Leader insight**
>
> *We need all managers to be committed to continuous learning and to be prepared to embrace change.*
>
> Sir David Nicholson, Chief Executive, NHS

Stand back and review progress

You need to stand above the fray and review the impact of change regularly. The vision can get very blurred at times, and it's all too easy to become lost in the detail or to lose sight of where you're heading.

Monitor and evaluate the results of the change programme against the goals and milestones established in the original plan. Are these goals still appropriate or do they need to be revised in the light of experience?

Existing performance measures may transmit the wrong signals and act as a block on change. Check that measures are consistent with the vision and goals, and if not, redesign them.

Be honest in your assessment of progress. If there is a real divergence between the planned goals and reality, take corrective action quickly. Be open about failure and involve employees in setting new targets or devising new measures.

Leader insight

Change produces discontinuity, which is a good thing. Clear action must be taken when systems are failing.

Lord Bichard, founder, Institute for Government

 Checklist: Implementing an effective change programme

- **Agree the implementation strategy:** The strategy needs to be clear before you begin to embark on change. Decide whether the implementation will be top-down, bottom-up or a mix of both. Also, consider whether to make the change by division, by department or in a 'big bang' approach.
- **Agree the time frame:** Every change programme needs a start date and a finite time span, regardless of whether it is being introduced incrementally or simultaneously across divisions. The timetable must be stretching enough to convey urgency, but attainable enough to be motivating.
- **Draw up detailed implementation plans:** Do this with each divisional or departmental head. Empower line managers to determine how they will implement the details of change against the overall goals. Ensure the strategy and goals behind the change programme are consistent with those behind any other corporate initiatives. Make sure employees are receiving consistent messages about the organisation's core values and beliefs from each of the programmes.

- **Set up a team of stakeholders:** The stakeholder team will not necessarily include top management, but will benefit from top management sponsorship. It will include the key people involved in designing and delivering the product or service, as well as those receiving it. The team will also be responsible for defining and disseminating the benefits of the change.

- **Manage with political awareness:** Often people complain about the politics in their roles because they are not practiced in managing the 'political' dimensions and the competing agendas. The CMI's diagnostic toolkit on leading with political awareness offers some valuable insights and practical advice.

- **Establish good project management:** Treat change like any project. Set goals and milestones, and monitor progress to keep the project on schedule and on budget. Flag up any potential problems as early as possible and make any necessary contingency plans. Establish the project team ground rules, particularly with regard to the areas of information-sharing, decision-making and reporting.

- **Communicate clearly:** The importance of good communications to the success of change programmes must not be underestimated. Communicate openly, honestly and above all regularly. Make sure you create an authentic two-way dialogue that genuinely welcomes employees' views and concerns.

- **Ensure participation:** Change can be stressful if imposed, so individual employees must feel that they can take ownership of the change programme as it evolves. Introduce mechanisms to facilitate this. Allow criticism and feedback, but ensure that corrective action can be taken where feedback suggests this is necessary.

- **Motivate:** Sustained change requires very high levels of motivation. People need to feel valued, to be developed, to have their achievements recognised and to be challenged. Recognise that different rewards will motivate different people to change.

- **Anticipate stress:** It is uncertainty rather than change that really worries employees. Provide as much information as possible and quash rumours as soon as they arise. Any change programme is stressful; fear of the unknown rather than change itself is the major contributory factor. Reduce its impact by being as open as possible about all the consequences of change. See that employees own the changes.

- **Remember that change is discontinuous:** Incremental change is a very long process, made up of very small and often invisible modifications to behaviour and attitudes. Seek innovative ways to remind staff of the overall case for change and to reinforce its value to them. Accept that change will be a stop/start process. Plan for this and develop strategies to gear the organisation up for renewed efforts when there are setbacks.

In this chapter we have looked at the rapid pace of organisational change and at the skills and techniques that managers need to lead their teams successfully in turbulent times. As you have read, gaining employee commitment for change is a key task. Building internal engagement is, however, only part of the picture. In Chapter 4 we go on to look at how the ability to manage a wide and complex range of stakeholders is rapidly becoming a vital management competency.

CHAPTER 4

Stakeholders don't expect us to be holier than Mother Teresa. They know we are in the business of making money; but they want us to do it in a responsible way.

Stephen Howard, Chief Executive, Business in the Community (BITC)

When a senior civil servant was recently asked how they would define success, it was in terms of the number of policy documents issued, green and white papers published, parliamentary questions answered and press releases issued.

On the surface, it might look as if this manager was performing well. What's missing, however, is any reference to many of the stakeholders in the organisation and what they would regard as a job well done.

It's a trap that many managers fall into and the reason behind many project and policy failures. They put their heads down and focus on the key tasks at the expense of thinking about how their job role fits into the bigger picture of the organisation and the people it's there to serve.

Managing stakeholders is more of an art than a science, and the ability to do it well has never been more important.

- The pace of globalisation and technological change means that organisations increasingly have to work in partnership with others to deliver what customers need.
- As the 'Berlin Wall' between the public, private and voluntary sectors comes down, we can expect to see more interaction and more examples of organisations joining forces to provide front-line services.
- Forward-looking organisations have also recognised that if managed effectively, shareholders can become advocates for the business and can help to drive growth.

The concept of stakeholder management is not new, but the idea that their interests should drive daily business decisions calls for a fundamental shift in thinking on the part of many managers. They are locked in the mindset of putting financial return for shareholders to the fore – which is of course the way many businesses have traditionally been managed.

This chapter looks at how managers who engage fully with their stakeholders can make better business decisions while also delivering bottom-line results. It gives guidance on how managers can gain a deeper insight into the perceptions and needs of key stakeholders and can harness their support and commitment to organisational goals. It provides practical tools to help managers map and communicate effectively with stakeholders, as well as insights from business leaders who have achieved great results by putting stakeholder concerns at the heart of their operation.

What is a stakeholder?

The Chartered Management Institute (CMI) defines a stakeholder as 'any person, or organisation, with a vested interest in the successful operation of a company or organisation.'

In practice, this means a stakeholder could be internal or external to the organisation. They may have a direct interest in the outcome or success of an initiative or business, or they may just occasionally come into contact with it. They could be an employee, customer, supplier, partner organisation or even the local community that a business operates in. Shareholders should also be regarded as stakeholders, but it's important to recognise the difference. Shareholders own part of the company; stakeholders have an interest in the business or organisation but do not own it.

It's often helpful to distinguish between primary and secondary stakeholder groups. Primary stakeholders define the business and are vital to its continued existence. So primary stakeholder groups might be:

- Customers
- Suppliers
- Employees
- Shareholders and investors.

Secondary stakeholders are those who may affect relationships with primary stakeholders. For example, an environmental pressure group may influence customers by suggesting that your products fail to meet eco-standards. Secondary stakeholders may include:

- Competitors
- Consumer groups
- Central or local government bodies
- The media
- Pressure groups
- Trade unions
- Community groups.

No two organisations will have exactly the same stakeholder groups. The list will vary enormously depending on the nature of the business and where and how it operates. Often stakeholders are 'hidden' or not fully recognised.

When a business fails, for example, it's not only the bank that loses its loan or a family that loses security; there will be a knock-on effect in the local community. When Woolworths, the department store, went to the wall in 2008, a big hole was left in many high streets. Shoppers used to relying on 'Woolies' felt both aggrieved and inconvenienced. Many family incomes suffered and the economic and social impact was much greater than the loss of profit to Woolworths plc. Clearly, the bigger the enterprise, the more stakeholders are affected.

Equally, the stakeholders in a major event such as the Olympic Games are many and varied. Everyone in the UK has a stake in the 2012 Games' success. Communities will be affected by the construction of the Olympic stadium sites but will also benefit from the resulting re-generation of their area. Many businesses will succeed or fail based on their involvement in the Games. Sport as a whole will benefit, as will the young people who will have access to better facilities. Although a one-off event, the ripple effect will be felt in the run up and in the aftermath, both positively and negatively, by many people.

Identifying your stakeholders

A critical first task for managers in any sector or discipline is to identify who their most important stakeholders are. This is not a job that should be done alone – it's important to involve people from across and outside the business to get a full picture. Focus groups, brainstorming sessions and interviews with key customers, partners and suppliers will all help to put the pieces of the puzzle together.

Once armed with the necessary information, it's a good idea to put together a stakeholder map. One way to do this is to construct a diagram with the organisation at the centre, primary stakeholders around it and secondary stakeholders in a different tier (see Figure 4.1).

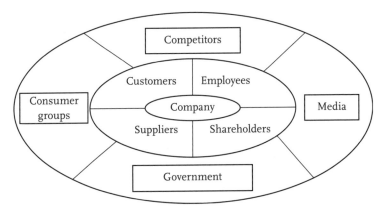

Figure 4.1 Stakeholder analysis and management

Prioritise your stakeholders

A power/interest grid can map the level of interest that different stakeholders have in the operations of your organisation and their power to affect it. This will help you to decide where you need to invest your stakeholder management efforts.

Clearly you will need to engage fully with those who have both a high level of interest and a high level of power, and take great care over relationships with these groups. You will want to keep those who have power but less interest satisfied, but not overwhelm them with too much information. Those with high interest but little power should be kept informed, but you won't need to pay so much attention to those with little interest and little influence. (See Figure 4.2.)

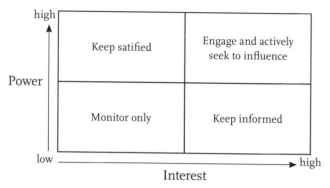

Figure 4.2 Stakeholder/interest matrix

Leader insight

You need to keep a close eye on key stakeholders, but the danger is you spend all your time window-gazing and getting distracted. Create a list of your priority stakeholders and keep in regular touch.

Phillippa Williamson, Chief Executive, Serious Fraud Office

Mapping interactions

Stakeholders often have complex interactions with each other. So it is a useful exercise to prepare a star diagram, as shown in Figure 4.3, to illustrate how they relate to each other.

Identifying the total list of stakeholders in an organisation and seeing where the links are can be an illuminating exercise. Even in a relatively straightforward business such as banking there are numerous parties with both complementary and conflicting interests. As well as shareholders and customers, for example, banks have a wide range of other stakeholders including building societies, companies, creditors, suppliers, the government, pensions funds, bond deals, investment

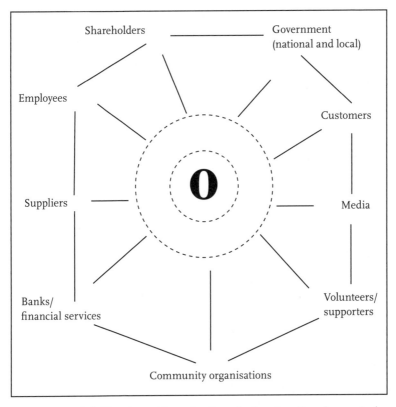

Figure 4.3 Stakeholders interactions. O = Organisation; its actions have a ripple effect. Also, various stakeholders impact and interact with each other

houses and a whole range of other financial institutions that are impacted directly by banking policy. The sheer interdependence of the institutions involved was a factor in explaining the impact which the collapse of only one bank could make on the system.

It's important to bear these close links between stakeholders in mind when you are planning any major new initiatives. Trading off the interests of one group of stakeholders against those of another is a risky strategy. Longer term, the interests of all stakeholders march together, so it is important to find creative solutions that satisfy the interests of everyone involved.

For example, BP's former CEO Tony Hayward did not fully understand that Congressmen were stakeholders in his business as well as the US President. He did not successfully manage his communications strategy with them and, as a result, paid a heavy price in the media coverage of BP.

Understanding stakeholders

Once you have acquired an understanding of who your stakeholders are, the next step is to try and develop an understanding of what they want from you. Stakeholders' expectations will be many and varied, so you need to evaluate what you know about their actual and previous behaviour and what underlies it.

A good technique is to put yourself in the place of each stakeholder and ask yourself what their perspective on your business may be. What are their needs and concerns? What affects or influences them? What do they believe? What motivates them? What potential threats or opportunities do they represent?

You need to think about their goals, the impact any organisational approach or initiative will have on them, and the likely extent of buy-in or level of support. Internal and external 'intelligence' and research will provide the answer to some of these questions, but one-to-one meetings or focus groups will help you develop a deeper knowledge of what makes your key stakeholders tick.

Once you have decided which stakeholders you most need to influence and have begun to understand what motivates them, you will be in a position to consider the way forward.

The following questions might help you develop strategies for action:

- How can you improve the products and services you offer to customers?

- Do you need to tailor your offering to different customer segments?
- How can you cooperate more effectively with suppliers?
- What will enhance the morale of your employees?
- What internal issues need to be resolved?
- What might encourage external stakeholders to be more cooperative?
- How can you change public perceptions of your organisation?
- Which policies or actions might run the risk of alienating stakeholders or increasing the threat they pose to your business?
- Which areas should you focus on?

Leader insight

Good managers and leaders focus on the things that matter. They know the numbers in their business but they are not driven by them. They draw on the contributions of all the business stakeholders and give them meaning.

Stephen Howard, Chief Executive, BITC

Dealing with conflicting demands

Stakeholder management can often be an uncomfortable process, where one set of needs must sometimes offset another. For example, ministers must make tough choices both practically and economically in the current public sector spending review. To do so requires a great deal of courage. They know they may only have a short window of opportunity before entrenched opposition starts to develop into a full-scale revolt. At the same time, they dare not risk a double-dip recession. Clear priorities need to be set for cutting spending while ensuring that critical services are still delivered.

In the private sector, conflict often emerges because of the differing needs and desires of stakeholders and shareholders. Shareholders, understandably, are looking for profit. Stakeholders often want to see decisions and actions taken that lead to more cost and therefore reduced profits. Business owners often have to tread a fine line between meeting their own needs and taking the desires of other stakeholders into account or they might risk losing their ability to generate future profits. An unpopular decision, for example, may lead to industrial action by employees or a boycott of products by customers.

It's important to recognise here that stakeholders can increase your risk as well as help you to maximise your opportunities. Often stakeholder management and risk management are regarded as two completely separate exercises – the two are, however, inextricably linked. In a multi-stakeholder environment it is worth plotting out who is taking the risk and outlining a strategy for managing any potential problems that may arise. Risks are usually more extensive when they are removed from the risk-taker – where a public service is contracted out to a third party, for example.

If you do contract with an outsourced supplier you can share the risk by the way you draft the contract, but you cannot reduce your accountability for the risk. This is an issue that needs more exploration as more public services are delivered by third parties. More detail about managing risk is provided in Chapter 5.

Leader insight

The stakeholders in the public sector are more complex. You have to try to second-guess a lot of other agendas. Inevitably, you sometimes get it wrong.

Calvert Markham, Managing Director, Elevation Learning

Managing stakeholder relationships

A strategic approach to managing stakeholder relationships is likely to yield the best results. A planned programme of communications will ensure that key messages are conveyed at the right time and that stakeholders feel both involved and informed.

This has to be a two-way street. It's an opportunity for the organisation to communicate its plans and harness support, but stakeholders will only become truly engaged if they have the chance to raise their concerns and make meaningful input.

Many organisations find an effective approach is to make a lead person responsible for communication with a key stakeholder or group of stakeholders – a bit like a key account manager in a sales or consultancy business.

It's not a 'one size fits all' approach: the method of communication has to be chosen carefully to suit the individual needs of different stakeholders and to tap into their existing communication channels. For example, when Tim Melville-Ross was CEO of Nationwide, he recognised that the media was a key stakeholder. He proactively befriended journalists to ensure they gave a more balanced view of Nationwide's actions during the downturn in the housing market in the early 1990s. He also recognised that he could tap into a new source of managerial talent by developing the mature female workforce into branch managers. This gave them a stake in the business and Nationwide the opportunity to capitalise on talent.

Some ideas you might like to consider include:

- One-to-one meetings
- Inviting stakeholders to sit on steering, advisory and working groups
- Inviting team members from stakeholder organisations to join you on secondment
- Joint working with stakeholder organisations on key issues

- Working groups or round table discussions where both parties can discuss key issues
- Written communication (newsletters, e-newsletters, targeted emails)
- Discussion/information groups on social media sites such as LinkedIn.

Leader insight

Be honest with people – even if there is bad news. If you tell the story straight, they will take it on board.

Sir John Sunderland, former Non-Executive Chairman, Cadbury Schweppes

The most successful organisations take their stakeholder relationships one step further by turning stakeholders into advocates rather than simply supporters. If stakeholders have a real understanding of what your organisation is trying to achieve, confidence in your ability to deliver and are satisfied that you will act in an appropriate and ethical manner, they can become your best ambassadors.

Case study: Champions and ambassadors

The Champion and Ambassador programmes run by Investors in People (IIP) and the CMI are both good examples of how stakeholders can be turned into advocates.

Investors in People is now a widely recognised kitemark for organisations that value their employees and invest in their continued development. Over the past 15–20 years, more than 33 000 corporate customers have paid a commercial price for the advice, assessment and recognition that leads to the standard being awarded.

Many household name businesses have been proud to display the quality brand, including Marks & Spencer, TNT, BBC, Nationwide, Ernst & Young, Innocent Drinks, The Carphone Warehouse, the Army, Navy and RAF, and nearly every major civil service department. By publicly displaying the brand these organisations become stakeholders in IIP rather than just customers. The 'Champions' programme was created to celebrate their contribution and effort, and to tap into the inspiration that they could provide to others.

IIP Champions deliver seminars, conferences and workshops to help spread the message about how the IIP standard can bring real business benefits and to share best practice on how to achieve it. IIP Ambassadors share their personal experiences of making the IIP journey happen in their organisation. They speak at events, provide comment to the press and take part in networking events so they can communicate the benefits of becoming an Investor in People.

The CMI also has an Ambassador programme. CMI members are stakeholders in the organisation: they don't own the business or have a financial stake in it, but if the CMI were to cease to exist tomorrow they would lose the ability through their professional body to keep their skills up to date and would miss out on other benefits such as access to the latest research, career counselling, mentoring and the ability to network with their peers.

The CMI's network of goodwill ambassadors are people from within the membership who are excellent managers and leaders, and who believe in the value of the CMI. They help to raise our profile by speaking at events and networking on our behalf across the UK.

It's a win-win situation. We acquire advocates who can demonstrate excellence in management and leadership, and promote the benefits of belonging to a professional association; they get the opportunity to raise their personal profile, build further on their presentation skills and receive mentoring from our high-profile Companions.

Ambassadors also get the opportunity to attend exclusive networking events, access cutting-edge research before anyone else and have use of all the CMI's online resources. It's an excellent example of how the stakeholder relationship can work both ways.

Reaping the rewards

Stakeholder management is undoubtedly a time-consuming and challenging task, but organisations who give it sufficient time and attention will reap the rewards in many and varied ways. Put simply, involving stakeholders can help organisations achieve better and faster results, whatever it is they may be trying to do.

Effective stakeholder management can help to:

- Generate repeat business
- Encourage innovation
- Lead to increased collaboration/partnership working
- Stimulate new policy approaches
- Expand marketing capability
- Increase sales
- Extend service delivery
- Maximise business opportunities.

Case study: The NSPCC

The National Society for the Prevention of Cruelty to Children (NSPCC) is an excellent example of how involving multiple stakeholders in critical decisions can lead to improved services.

In the early 1990s, the NSPCC embarked on a major strategic review. The aim was to find ways of delivering better services for children and families at a time when funding and voluntary income were in decline.

Key stakeholders – including social services, police forces, volunteers, staff and other regional children's charities – were involved in the exercise, and invited to contribute their views on what the NSPCC's focus should be.

As a result of the discussions, a new strategy based on 'prevention' was developed. This called for profound internal change, but also created new opportunities for the NSPCC to work in partnership with many of its stakeholders.

Close alliances were forged with organisations such as National Children's Homes (NCH) as well as with local government and social services departments. At the same time, the NSPCC developed its own child protection helpline, working alongside the police and healthcare professionals. The result was that the NSPCC became woven into the fabric of child protection and was able to move away from its image as a 19th century institution that sat uneasily alongside social services.

While it is difficult to quantify how much child abuse has been prevented, very few people would argue against prevention as a proper focus for resources. By providing help to vulnerable adults, a safer environment was created in homes where children were at risk. This led to less rather than more reliance on 'extreme' social services, who in the past had often appeared too late in the day to piece together fractured families in underprivileged communities. The old images of inspectors removing children by force from their abusive parents were replaced by child and adult centres that provided support but did not stigmatise or label families. The reach of services was extended beyond 'problem families' in a bid to shift the focus to good parenting.

This radical turn-around was made possible by the inclusion of all stakeholders in the debate about the future of the NSPCC. The exercise not only led to improved services and more efficient use of resources, but also acted as the catalyst for a whole new approach to safeguarding children.

Monitoring and review

One final point is that stakeholder management is not a static process. Organisations do not stand still; and equally, the influence and interests of stakeholder groups will change over time.

Stakeholder relationships need to be reviewed on a regular basis to take account of changing situations. Strategies for communication and involvement should be revisited and updated where necessary.

Take as an example the 2010 General Election. The result was a defeat for the Labour Party and the new leader Ed Milliband has taken the opportunity to reconnect with the party's grassroots and conduct a major policy review. This gives him the opportunity to jettison some of the past policies that had proved to be electorally unpopular and to put his own stamp on the party. However, he will need to gain some consensus during the review, establishing credibility across the party. He will also need to take into account the way the Conservative–Liberal Democrat coalition government is performing and the way the economy does (or does not) respond.

Key questions

- Have you shared your list of stakeholders with at least two other internal and external colleagues to make sure you have a full picture?
- Do you have a clear understanding of the needs and expectations of your stakeholders?
- Do you have an up-to-date understanding of how your stakeholders view your current performance and what they regard as your strengths and weaknesses?
- Do you know if and how the requirements of your stakeholders are likely to change over the next 12 months?
- How often do you communicate with stakeholders?
- Have you worked with them to develop a plan that will address their needs?
- Do your stakeholders feel they have access to you?
- Do you always follow up on queries or complaints?
- Do you acknowledge the successes of your stakeholders?
- Do you have a clear lead person internally for each external stakeholder?
- Is the lead person appraised on the basis of their stakeholder management?
- Have you ever lost the support of a key stakeholder? Did you ask why?

In this chapter we have looked at some of the practical tools managers can draw on to help them engage effectively with stakeholders. As you have read, putting stakeholders concerns at the heart of operations is the key to achieving great results. Managing stakeholders effectively can also help organisations reduce levels of corporate risk. In Chapter 5 we look in detail at the role that managers at all levels have to play when managing risk and ensuring business continuity.

CHAPTER 5

Don't assume people always understand the risks they are taking, particularly in respect of complicated or financial procedures.
Phillippa Williamson, Chief Executive, Serious Fraud Office

It's hard to pick up a newspaper these days without coming across yet another example of the consequences of poor management of corporate risk. In the past two years alone we have seen previously unsullied corporate reputations damaged beyond repair and household-name businesses we regarded as solid as a rock going to the wall.

It is clear there is not just a lack of preparedness, but also some real failings in the way that UK plc is currently managing organisational risk. This is borne out by recent Chartered Management Institute (CMI) research that shows that fewer than half of UK organisations are proactively practising business continuity management.

Two fundamental problems lie at the heart of this issue. First, organisational motivations for managing risk have become somewhat skewed. Evidence suggests that it is the need to demonstrate good corporate governance that is driving risk management in organisations rather than the desire to sustain good organisational performance and maintain services.

We seem to have got into a mindset where risk management is about compliance and about spotting and fixing problems. Managers haven't fully woken up to the fact that, applied effectively, it is a key business tool that can actually help organisations improve performance and identify and exploit new opportunities.

Getting the balance right is not easy. Pay too little attention to risk and problems will creep up and take you unawares. Becoming too risk-averse, on the other hand, can have a placebo effect and stifle progress and creativity.

One of the key themes emerging from the leader interviews conducted in writing this book is that risk registers can be overly repetitive. They are also dangerous if the register becomes the outcome rather than a management tool. Risk must be managed on a daily basis and the key corporate risks need to be monitored by the most senior leaders. Most importantly of all, the identifiable risk should always be accompanied by a risk register strategy and action planning.

Managers need help in making sure that the scales don't tip too far in either direction – and herein lies the second problem. Organisations are simply not preparing their managers adequately for the task of managing risk and ensuring business continuity.

The ultimate responsibility for risk management must, of course, lie at the very top of the organisation. But a culture of appropriate risk management has to be embedded throughout the business and involve managers from all disciplines and at all levels.

Managing risk isn't just the preserve of the specialist risk management team (if indeed there is one) or of the IT or facilities people. It's a cross-functional activity that increasingly needs to involve managers from areas such as HR, marketing and public relations too. As a manager, you need to develop the antennae to sense potential problems, the ability to understand the implications of their actions and decisions, and the confidence to raise the alarm if they see things going wrong.

In this chapter we look at the diverse risks emerging in today's complex business environment and highlight the need for forward planning and speedy responses. We also look at some of the latest research on business continuity planning and the proactive strategies that managers can take to mitigate risk and improve their ability to manage it on a day-to-day basis.

Leader insights

One person's risk will create another person's opportunity.

Charles Tilley, Chief Executive, Chartered Institute of Management Accountants (CIMA)

Work on risk is very challenging because it is easy to get things wrong. If you are too low-risk you will miss opportunity. If you try ideas out and they are well constructed with strong internal leaders and external partnerships and support, you can reduce your risk significantly and still build a growth strategy.

Martin Bean, Vice Chancellor, The Open University

What do we mean by 'risk'?

The risks likely to affect businesses can generally be broken down into three broad areas (courtesy of *Instant Manager: Managing Change*, CMI, Bernice Walmsey, 2009):

- **Financial:** This includes things such as the risk of a large customer going out of business while they owe money to the company or fraud by an employee. Of course all organisations are also subject to the risks from the trade cycle, or crises in financial markets – as the experience of the last few years has graphically shown. A current business risk may well be social unrest, as we see the impact of the government's cuts in public sector expenditure taking effect during 2011.

- **Operational:** This includes types of risk that will affect an organisation's ability to produce the goods and services that are at the centre of its business. Examples of this type of risk include breakdown of a vital piece of machinery or the inability of employees to get in to work because of severe weather or a flu pandemic.
- **Market-based:** These risks emerge from developments in the market that the company operates in. An example would be if market demand changes substantially or if a new competitor enters the arena.

It's important to recognise that risk does not remain static; there is always the potential for new risk to emerge. In its report *Management Futures*, the CMI looked at what the business landscape might look like in the future. It came up with no less than 17 scenarios that organisations might be faced with in 2018, including a business world under cyber-attack, the remote (yet feasible) use of microchip implants to control employee behaviour and an increasingly isolated US withdrawing from the world economy.

Risk in reality

Another CMI report, *Disruption and Resilience: The 2010 Business Continuity Management Survey*, paints an interesting picture of what managers perceive as the biggest business risks compared to what caused the most disruption over the past 12 months in reality.

For the first time extreme weather was the most commonly experienced disruption, surpassing disruption caused by the loss of IT, which had topped the table in previous years.

Loss of people remains the third most widely experienced disruption (28%), emphasising the need to take people issues into account when assessing risk and to avoid a purely technological approach. Another notable area of growth is experiencing damage to corporate brand, which doubled from 11 to 22%. This highlights the fact that organisations need to pay attention to reputation and brand risk as well as operational risk. (We talk more about managing reputation in Chapter 8.)

When managers were asked to identify what they perceived to be the biggest threats facing their organisation, loss of IT and loss of telecommunications came out on top, reflecting the increasing reliance of organisations on their ICT infrastructure. Inability to access work sites or buildings was also highlighted as a major concern.

Although there had been major concerns about disruption from swine flu, and many organisations had taken action to limit its spread, this was not borne out in reality. In fact only 3% described the disruption caused by employee illness as significant. By comparison, more than 80% of organisations experienced some disruption as a result of postal strikes, which they were much less prepared for.

Risk in good times and bad

Managers were also asked how the recession had affected their organisation's overall attitude to risk. While one-third reported that they had become more risk-averse, more than half of respondents said their risk appetite had not changed. One in ten reported that their risk appetite had actually increased.

While the potential risks presented by an economic downturn are blatantly obvious, it is important to understand that risks accrue as a result of rapid periods of economic growth too. In these conditions, there is a tendency for individuals to over-stretch themselves and for organisations to try to do too many things at once. The cost base expands very quickly to meet demand and people are added to the payroll as the fastest way of growing the company. Wages and salaries rise not because performance has improved, but because the market has grown. Everyone has the feel-good factor.

These are heady circumstances and it is only over the long term that we can see the wider implications. Costs are too high and expectations of income growth stimulate higher levels of borrowing and spending. This can only go on for so long until the bubble bursts and the business is forced to get back to focusing on productivity again.

The CMI's view is that measuring productivity is vital in both good times and bad. It is the only way a business can tell, first, whether performance is improving at all, and second, whether it is improving by a sufficient margin to allow the business to remain competitive.

It is surprising that so few companies do this on a systematic basis, given that it would be fairly easy to measure and benchmark against sector and industry standards. Just as 35 of the Fortune 500 companies in the US voluntarily report on their carbon footprint, so UK companies should report annually on the returns that they are achieving on capital and people employed. This would help them measure their successes, evaluate when the revenue looks unstable and weak, and take corrective action. It is an efficient way of managing risk and uncertainty while maintaining a clear focus on adding value.

Risk in the public sector

Managing risk is of course not just the preserve of the private sector; it is just as important in our public services. Nobody wants the local hospital or school to close because the money has run out. Yet the management of risk in the public sector is not as good as it could be.

There is a tendency to downplay risk because in public sector occupations there is a perceived 'protection' from the worst vagaries of the market. This era of protected public revenues is of course coming to an end. Public procurement, compulsory competitive tendering and increasing overlaps between public/private provision do mean that risk management ought to be a shared discipline across the two sectors and that, increasingly, risk ought to be managed holistically rather than project by project.

For example, when Camden Local Authority outsourced all its child protection to the NSPCC, it still needed a risk strategy that both parties owned. Similarly, Crossrail is publicly funded but relies on a range of private sector providers. The management of contracts and the risks within them will be key to the delivery of the Crossrail project as a whole.

It's important to acknowledge, however, that public sector managers are working in a very complex environment. The ability to manage risk is often not in the skill set of busy teachers, social workers or police officers, and much more resource will have to be pumped into their development if they are to acquire the sophisticated level of skill required.

Creating the right culture for risk management

Two factors explain why some organisations are better at managing risk than others:

- An organisational culture that is open and honest
- A high level of management skills and competency.

There is no doubt that the ultimate responsibility for risk sits at senior level, but it should not be the preserve of the few. Risk management has to be a cross-functional activity and an area where all managers are encouraged to take ownership and responsibility. Organisations need to develop a cadre of risk-aware managers who can manage risk systematically on a day-to-day basis and who will have the necessary courage to take action and blow the whistle if necessary.

RBS is an example of what can happen if these factors are not in place. This was an organisation with great HR practices, a charismatic CEO and an impressive history of growth in the 1990s. In the end, however, RBS had a risk propensity that was culturally acceptable and embedded, and it took far too much risk with clients' money. When middle-ranking managers tried to blow the whistle they were not noticed. No one listened; they were too busy calculating how to earn bigger and bigger bonuses.

The non-executive board was not operating to rational lending ratios. They were not sufficiently risk-averse and they were not prepared when the bubble burst. They had the added disadvantage of grossly inflated senior executive salaries and a perception that nothing could go wrong. It could be argued that in a more open culture, with better trained and more empowered middle managers, RBS may not have collapsed so spectacularly and could have been saved.

The opposite side of the coin is illustrated by the example of Cadbury in the 1980s when it went through a merger with Schweppes and became the holding company for a number of major high street brands. It went through the pain of restructuring and cost reduction but it came out on top and intact. The philosophy of management was very different. Relationships with the workforce were more open and honest. The competence of middle managers was very good. The changes were well planned and implemented. Risks were minimised in the broader interest and were not simply defined in terms of shareholder value.

A key part of creating the right culture is also to incentivise good behaviour. Organisations need to make it clear what kind of behaviours are expected, and to reward managers appropriately for displaying them. This will help to drive good performance, which will in turn lead to less risk over the longer term.

Leader insight

I don't believe that currently risk management is embedded in our approach to management and leadership. We have a really big productivity challenge. The old certainties are not there any more and I think managing risk is about having a more emotionally and intellectually mature workforce who are prepared to change and manage risk.

Sir David Nicholson, Chief Executive, NHS

Key skills for managers

So what are the skills that managers and leaders need to help them manage risk effectively? The following list will help you benchmark your own competence and highlight the areas where development might be needed for yourself or your team:

- **Good anticipation:** How far are you looking ahead? How good is your intelligence? What risks are you taking now and how might those risks increase? What relationships are key to minimising risk? How will we deal with the burden of regulation?
- **Communication skills:** You will not be able to manage risks without these. Communication skills will help you make sure your risk avoidance strategy is robust and understood.
- **Political awareness:** This will help you sense concerns. It's about having the willingness to listen and heed warnings from above and below, and from one's broader connections with key stakeholders, and an understanding of the wider business environment.
- **Financial knowledge and the skills to handle complex data:** It's no good plotting and planning based on an insufficient understanding of the cost and revenue drivers in your business; understanding what is driving your profit line and how competitive you are in the market place is the critical factor. Once this knowledge is shared and disseminated through all the managers in the business, risks can be mitigated and managed. Genuine opportunities for growth can be spotted and the right strategies for implementation can be deployed. However, you need a person who thinks numerically and understands the business thoroughly near the top of the organisation, otherwise you are flying blind.
- **Planning capability:** You always need a plan A, plan B and plan C. If you are always assuming 100% implementation of the business plan, with no downside or upside contingencies, then your business plan is too risky. It may be entirely right, but you have no risk manage-

ment strategy in place. Don't set your sights too low, however, or you may not have a business left at all. Your plan B must be realistic and aspirational, with contingencies built in from the start. There also ought to be triggers for action – for example, in a charity, if reserves fall below the three-month level, you will almost certainly need to make cuts.

Many senior managers do not necessarily have these skills, or they are tempted to cascade responsibility to far too low a level. This is a huge mistake. Big corporate/public sector risks must always be managed at the top, with a full understanding of the potential consequences.

Leader insights

We need to educate people on how to manage risk, e.g. we need organisations to ask themselves regularly, if so and so happened, how would the organisation handle it? Sometimes, by asking the right question, you can encourage the right behaviours, but you will never eliminate risk. If we eliminate risk, we also eliminate creativity and innovation.

Vicky O'Dea, Operations Director, Serco

We need to manage fixed and variable costs and look ahead. It's not just about the banking community. Lots of managers and leaders were caught napping.

Calvert Markham, Managing Director, Elevation Learning

Business continuity management

A framework for managing corporate risk on a day-to-day basis is provided by the practice of business continuity management (BCM). Put simply, BCM is based on the principle that one of the key responsibilities of an organisation's directors is to ensure the continuation of business operations at all times.

In the wider context, BCM is an established part of the UK's preparations for possible threats posed to organisations, whether from internal systems failures or external emergencies such as extreme weather, terrorism or infectious disease.

Frontline responders, such as the emergency services, are required to conduct BCM under the UK's Civil Contingencies Act 2004, while since 2006, local authorities have been obliged to both practice BCM themselves and to promote it to the business and voluntary organisations that operate in their communities. In 2008, the Pitt Review on the flooding emergencies of June and July 2007 recommended that BCM should be more widely implemented by infrastructure providers.

Practice of BCM among organisations, however, remains low. The CMI's 'Disruption and Resilience' survey suggests that fewer than half of organisations have a formal business continuity plan (BCP). Larger organisations were more than twice as likely to have dedicated BCPs than smaller organisations (65% compared to 29%). The practice of BCM is most common in the public sector, followed by public limited companies. The proportion of charity/not-for-profit organisations with a BCP stands at 51%, while private limited companies have the lowest level of take-up.

There are extensive differences across sectors. Finance, insurance and health and social care sectors are more likely, for example, to have BCPs than organisations from the transport and logistics, manufacturing and production, or business services sectors.

The British Standard for BCM, BS25999, provides guidance for organisations on how to develop and implement BCM within the business. A supplementary specification, which has been available since 2007, provides a framework for demonstrating compliance via an auditing and certification process. Only 14% of organisations in the CMI survey report use BS25999, although 41% of managers are aware of the standard.

BCM can:

- Help to identify potential risks across all areas of an organisation's operations
- Improve the ability to forward-plan
- Help managers make better decisions at times of crisis
- Reduce the amount of time spent on emergency action
- Help organisations manage resources more efficiently
- Prevent serious disruption to services.

Case study: BCP at Xchanging

Xchanging is a fast-growing, pure-play global business processor that provides complex, industry-specific processing services to blue chip customers. Because the services they provide to their clients are so critical, they have effective BCM processes and procedures in place.

In January 2010 Xchanging's Leadenhall Street offices in London, where 560 staff are employed, were affected by a power outage. When power was subsequently restored to the area a power surged damaged the internal power equipment. The disruption occurred at 10 a.m. but, despite the efforts of engineers, by 4 p.m. only 50% of the floors in the building had a stable power supply.

A decision was made to invoke their work area recovery contract with ICM Continuity Services and make arrangements to move staff to the London City Business Continuity Centre in Wapping. Xchanging had in place a recovery contract for several hundred seats at the facility and it was decided that a phased approach to the recovery would be implemented, with 100 seats being made live initially. Four hours later a fully functioning facility was up and running, and available to staff to use the following morning. Xchanging's email system (key to their business operations) was not affected by the power outage, because a back-up email system was hosted at the ICM Business Continuity Centre that automatically provided service.

Nigel Knight, Head of BCM for Xchanging, stressed the importance of having work area recovery contracts to protect key business operations. He emphasised that it is essential to regularly exercise BCPs and actually involve operational staff by moving them to the recovery centre. It was this policy of regular exercising that made the invocation so successful.

In the event the power to the Leadenhall building was fully restored before the start of the next day and ICM's London City facility was stood down.

Putting BCM into practice

A strategic approach to managing risk definitely pays dividends. In the CMI's survey, 79% of managers who had activated their BCP in the previous 12 months agreed that it had effectively reduced the impact of disruption.

Managing risk means thinking about what might go wrong and putting strategies in place to try and minimise the effect on the business. It's simply not feasible, however, to plan for the hundreds of specific 'disasters' that might occur. A more valuable approach is to think about what you need to do to get up and running again in the event of a crisis.

In other words, it really doesn't matter if it's fire or flood that has brought your operation to a halt – what's important is that your IT system has gone down and you can't communicate with customers or fulfil orders. The key is to identify what are the absolutely essential things you have to do to get it back in place quickly.

Leader insight

You can't have a plan for every eventuality. What you need to do is identify what are the absolutely key things you have to do if for any reason your business is interrupted, and then look at how you could get them back in place quickly.

John Sharp, business continuity expert, quoted in *Professional Manager* magazine

Of course it's not just operational risk that needs to be planned for – reputational risk is equally important. One of the worst impacts on shareholder value is caused by unexpected dips in productivity and performance. Markets can cope well with trailed news, particularly if they see effective action being taken. What they don't like is a bolt from the blue. Even modest losses that are not anticipated or, worse still, show no evidence that managers and leaders are taking a grip of the situation can be very damaging.

Stories to illustrate this point abound. Just take a look at the share price of BP in recent months: all the time the oil was leaking into the Gulf of Mexico, BP was leaking shareholder value. The price of shares only rallied when BP's management took a clear line of action.

In these circumstances, clear action and a decisive and firm approach to the world's media is critical to managing the situation. An important lesson for managers and leaders is to take responsibility and be very clearly visible during the moment of crisis.

Driving BCM through the supply chain is also important for any organisation wishing to improve its resilience. An organisation is only as resilient as the external stakeholders it relies on. So how do you ensure they don't let you down? What kind of incentives do they have in order to perform to your standards?

Key questions to ask your business-critical suppliers and outsourcing partners are:

- Who is the senior manager responsible for your organisation's BCM?
- Do you have BCPs that cover all the products and services we source from you?
- When was your BCP last used and what were the results?
- What actions have been taken to incorporate lessons from BCP exercises?
- When were your BCM processes last audited?

 Checklist

- **Define scope and objectives:** Define and agree the scope and objectives of the BCP. Because business continuity includes many interdependent elements, limits of responsibility must be agreed. It is essential that senior management support, and have ownership of, the business continuity process. Appoint a champion on the senior management team and ensure that they understand their role in setting policy and in ensuring that the plan is adopted and maintained throughout the organisation. A team with cross-function experience and sufficient seniority should be appointed to manage the planning process. Overall business objectives must be clear. Objectives may be set based upon a number of pre-determined high-level failures or change scenarios, such as equipment or network service failures, loss of essential services, denial of access to premises, supply chain disruption, significant staff changes, or any combination of failures.
- **Gain an understanding of your business:** In order to plan effectively for potential disruptions you need as complete a picture of your organisation as is possible. Identify:
  - The key products and services of the business that generate the most revenue and profit

- The critical processes and resources involved in production or in delivering the service
- The personnel who are critical to the activity
- The 'gatekeepers' of knowledge within the organisation
- Your main suppliers and the risks they may be taking
- The critical elements in the supply chain
- Your main customers and their areas of business activity.

- **Assess risks:** Conducting a risk assessment provides the basic information necessary to evaluate potential continuity arrangements and to prioritise their implementation. Generally, risk analysis is based upon two criteria (likelihood of failure and business impact of failure), although a third criterion (the period of failure) may also be considered. Many organisations can sustain service failures for short periods without a critical business impact. A questioning approach is a good way of gaining the information needed to assess risk. Ask:

  - 'What if' questions – what if our IT network went down? What if a fire destroyed key documents? What if a key member of staff is off ill? What if our main supplier could not supply us? What if a customer could not pay us?
  - What is the worst-case scenario? A worst case is most likely something that would halt your business completely. Think about cause and effect, and how a chain of events might develop from just one incident.
  - What functions and people are critical? Some work is more essential to the business than others. Part of the business continuity process is to identify who needs to do what, when and where immediately after a failure or incident.

- **Evaluate potential continuity arrangements:** Once the risk analysis is complete, you need to evaluate potential continuity arrangements. Usually this is carried out in order of priority, as defined by the risk analysis. Each of the potential continuity arrangements should be considered in terms of cost and benefit, and the likely timescale for delivery. Positive and negative aspects of each option are considered and the best options to meet the defined objective selected.

- **Define your strategy:** Once you have identified and evaluated the risks and potential continuity arrangements, you need board-level agreement on the business tasks that are essential. It may be that the board takes a different view over priorities from departmental heads. You need to establish firm priorities and ensure that all departments buy into the plan. For each identified risk you can decide to:
  - Accept the risk and take no further action
  - Attempt to reduce or eliminate the risk
  - Attempt to reduce the risk and develop continuity solutions should the incident occur
  - Stop, suspend or re-engineer the process where the risk cannot be eliminated.
- **Develop your BCPs:** An effective BCP should aim to explain who needs to do what, who takes responsibility and who deputises for key roles. It should use checklists and flow charts to explain key activities that need to be taken to restore key products and services within the agreed timescales and to the agreed levels. BCPs should be designed to provide clear, short instructions of how to carry out the necessary elements of the plan, together with any system/service and contact information. It should be remembered that only essential information is required at times of crisis.
- **Exercise and review:** The business continuity plan should be reviewed and rehearsed on a regular basis. Rehearsals will help familiarise the team with the procedures and highlight any problem areas. Based upon the results of the exercises, the continuity provisions, procedures and plans should be amended as necessary.

Case study: Chelsea Building Society

(Extreme weather is now top of the list of potential risks facing business. This case study, reproduced from the March 2008 issue of *Professional Manager* magazine, looks at how Chelsea Building Society managed to keep the wheels turning when it was faced with major disruption caused by an unprecedented level of flooding.)

It was a Friday in July and Adam Evetts was sitting in his office at Chelsea Building Society in Cheltenham, watching as the water rose slowly but surely up the flood defences he could see from his window.

As divisional director of risk for the organisation, he was on alert for the possibility of flooding, but certainly wasn't expecting the magnitude of the disaster that was about to strike.

Over the weekend, water levels rose to an unprecedented level, flooding homes, businesses and major local road networks, resulting in untold damage and disruption. Amidst all the chaos and confusion, a further crisis began to unfold. The Severn Trent Water Authority's Mythe Water Treatment Works was flooded, leaving 350 000 people in the surrounding area without clean running water.

Chelsea Building Society's incident management team met early on the Monday morning to assess the situation. The premises were intact, but they were still faced with an enormous challenge. Namely, how to keep the business operational at probably its busiest time of year, while dealing with the health and safety ramifications presented by around 700 people working in offices without running water or flushing toilets.

To compound the situation, many of the building society's staff were either mopping up at home or struggling to cope without water for drinking, cooking and washing themselves. There was also a knock-on effect for those with family responsibilities, as many of the local schools and nurseries had been forced to close their doors.

'We were faced with a situation where we had to make it more attractive for people to come to work than to want to stay at home – and that became the focus of what we were trying to do,' explained Evetts.

Identifying priorities

The incident management team identified those areas of the business that were non-essential in a crisis situation and pulled together a team of around 15 volunteers to run errands and generally support their efforts.

Getting hold of as much bottled water as possible was a priority, and with rationing already in place at local supermarkets, some volunteers were dispatched outside the area to gather stocks. Supplies of sandwiches were brought in to help keep staff going, while members of the senior management team went round the building with a morale-boosting chocolate trolley.

'The chocolate trolley became a daily feature,' said Evetts. 'It meant senior managers were able to keep people up-to-date with what we were doing here, ask how they were getting on at home, and it helped to create an atmosphere that we genuinely cared about our staff and their well-being.'

As it became apparent the situation was going to continue for days, perhaps even weeks, sourcing an ongoing supply of water became a priority. Organising a 25 000 gallon tanker of water to come up from Dorset wasn't too much of a problem; the much bigger issue facing the team was how to get it stored and pumped round the building when it arrived.

The majority of staff work in a Regency building with header tanks in the loft. The team managed to hire a fire engine from Lincolnshire and, with some rapid training provided by two personnel from the Fire Service College at nearby Moreton-in-Marsh, the water was pumped up to the header tanks.

'One of our risk guys documented the training and produced a mini-training course that anyone who was going to touch the fire engine had to complete,' explained Evetts. 'We didn't go near any of the high-pressure tools, but we were able to master the basics so that we could pump water to where we needed it.'

With flushing toilets (supplemented by a few Portaloos) now back in place, business almost as usual became a reality. As an additional incentive to staff to keep coming to work, the team also managed to come to an arrangement with a conference centre just outside the county who were willing to share shower facilities. An online booking service was quickly set up so that staff and their families were able to book half-hour slots to have a welcome wash and brush up.

The people factor

'It was the small things that became important to keep people coming into work,' said Evetts. 'As soon as we were able to demonstrate to staff that we cared about them and their environment, they were more willing to do anything we asked for, and many people went beyond the call of duty.'

The significance of the people factor in business continuity is probably the most important lesson Chelsea learned from the entire incident. 'Business continuity tends to be a paper-driven exercise, focusing on the physical aspects like the building and IT equipment,' says Evetts. 'But what we found in a crisis is that the building is nothing without the people in it. There's an assumption that people will be there − but the reality is this has affected them and their personal and home lives as well, so you have to factor that human element into your plans.'

Chelsea's determination to stay true to its core values also helped it keep going despite the mayhem that was going on all around. 'I think it is vital you don't forget what is important to you as an organisation and that you try and stick to what you stand for, as opposed to saying it's a crisis and your values don't apply,' says Evetts.

He adds that good communication was vital in building the 'gung ho' spirit that kept the business able to service its customers (with virtually no disruption) throughout the eight days. A decision was taken early on to issue updates to staff every one and a half hours, so that everyone knew exactly what the organisation was doing, as well as what developments there had been in the situation outside.

Crisis management

Chelsea's post-incident evaluation also highlighted a number of issues around the make-up and operation of a crisis management team. Having a group of people who gelled together well and were able to be inventive in finding solutions, for example, was key in helping the building society stay calm in a crisis. A short-term strategy, as well as a long-term one, helped the team focus on immediate priorities, while regular feedback sessions at the beginning and end of each day allowed people to keep in touch and identify any issues.

As a result of the incident, the organisation has made a major shift in the way it views its business continuity planning. 'There is quite a different focus now to our planning to make it far more flexible so it can cope with these unforeseen things,' says Evetts. 'One of the key lessons we learned is that no crisis is going to be exactly as you thought it would be, and no two crises are ever going to be the same, so you have to be reactive to that.'

Ongoing monitoring

Systems for identifying and managing risk have to be regularly monitored and reviewed to make sure they are reflecting changes in the business or the wider environment. Rehearsals are a fundamental aspect of good BCM practice, enabling plans to be revised, refined and updated before weaknesses are exposed by a real disruption.

In the CMI survey, just under half of managers whose organisations had BCPs reported that they exercise their plans once or more per year. Seventy per cent of those who had rehearsed their BCP said the rehearsal had exposed shortcomings in their plan. Often the shortcomings that are highlighted can be easily addressed. For example, a health and social care manager sharing their experience of BCP rehearsals commented that 'in our BCP rehearsal for electricity loss, the back-up generator did not operate. As a result we were able to replace the unit and prevent further disruption.'

The survey showed that organisations were adopting a variety of rehearsal formats. Seventy-three per cent performed 'table-top' exercises, 44% conducted IT back-up exercises and 22% played out full emergency scenarios.

Key questions

- Who is the senior manager responsible for your organisation's BCM?
- Do you have BCPs covering all your main procurement lines?
- What rewards are there in your culture for people who always deliver on time and to budget?
- What lessons are being learnt across the organisation every time there is an unanticipated change in the market or an outside variable that changes cost/projected returns?
- Are there any external benchmarks being delivered or used to improve the BCP's response times and outcomes?
- Do you have a management leadership development programme that focuses on BCM and BCPs?

In this chapter we have suggested some practical measures that managers can take to help them manage risk more effectively. As you have read, proactive management of risk is not just about compliance – it can also help organisations improve performance and exploit new opportunities. In Chapter 6 we go on to look at the environment, an area of potential risk that, if managed appropriately, can also offer great opportunity.

CHAPTER 6

Managing for the long term involves conserving resources rather than maximising short-term growth. All managers need to be encouraged to do this.

Stefan Stern, Director of Strategy, Edelman

As recently as a decade ago, the environmental agenda was regarded by many organisations as a fringe issue.

Very few UK executives would have seen environmental issues as having an influence on their day-to-day decisions. Even fewer would have recognised that tackling green issues could actually add value to the business in real terms.

How different things are today: the urgency of addressing climate change and depletion of the earth's resources is now universally recognised. After years of discussion and debate, there is now widespread acceptance that we need to make fundamental and far-reaching changes in the way we produce and consume products and services.

Management practice, however, does not appear to have kept pace with this shift in thinking. Too few organisations are taking the urgent action needed to significantly reduce their carbon footprint. They may be tinkering around the edges – recycling their paper and turning the lights out – but they have not recognised the need to make 'green' behaviour an integral part of everything they do. Research conducted by the Chartered Management Institute (CMI) shows that the environment is still very much a 'side' issue rather than a concern that is driving the business strategy and influencing the way organisations perceive and go about their business.

There is an urgent need to bring environmental management into the mainstream. It can no longer be regarded as a job that is outsourced to specialists or given to an enthusiast in addition to their day job.

Organisations need leaders and managers who have a clear understanding of how to proactively manage with the environment in mind. They need people who recognise that it is not just about reducing waste and saving money, but about developing and disseminating management practices that will help us make better use of finite resources. It will be interesting to see if the recession acts as a catalyst for more action. The need for financial savings may indeed compel organisations to educate their employees about environmental best practice.

This chapter looks at some of the latest research on how UK plc can become more 'lean and green' and provides practical guidance to help managers take a more sustainable approach to their work.

Leader insight

Businesses must make a reality of the concept of sustainable development, integrating the triple bottom line of environmental protection, social concern and economic success. It is disappointingly easy to argue that we have not been meeting any of these aspects. If the recession raises complex questions about the viability of economic models based on debt, it is worth remembering that environmentally, borrowing from the future is decidedly unsustainable.

Petra Wilton, Director of Policy and Research, CMI

Sustainable development – a critical role for businesses

The World Commission on Environment and Development report (commonly known as the Brundtland Commissions Report of 1987) coined the term 'sustainable development' and defined it as development 'that meets this generation's needs without compromising the ability of future generations to meet their own needs'.

The need for sustainability to be at the heart of our thinking is driven by three massive global issues:

- The depletion of the earth's resources, which has already happened through population growth and patterns of consumption
- The rapid economic growth that is anticipated among the most populated areas of the earth
- The growing problem of climate change.

None of these problems will go away without concerted action to tackle them. The urgent need for action has been underlined by a recent report showing that 30 million people are being affected globally by climate change. As Stern pointed out in his report to the UK government (*The Stern Review of the Economics of Climate Change*), the costs of action now are far outweighed by the damage that could be done to the fragile eco-structure that we all depend on.

The Brundtland report explicitly stated that businesses should take a positive role in environmental protection and argued they should become part of the solution rather than part of the problem. There are some interesting tensions inherent in this. Take the issue of energy, for example, where businesses have a Janus-like role. On the one hand they are greedy consumers of scarce resources; on the other, they are capable of driving the innovation in process, design and manufacturing that could have a radical impact on energy usage, transport, waste management and our pollution of the environment.

It will be interesting to see the impact of the financial penalties being imposed on businesses as part of the government's Carbon Reduction Commitment, which was introduced in April 2010. It will undoubtedly drive people's views on how they use energy within their organisations as we move towards the UK's target of an 80% reduction in carbon emissions by 2050.

There is, however, still a long way to go – as the CMI's report *Lean and Green: Leadership for the Low Carbon Economy* shows.

Current practice

Lean and Green is based on a UK-wide survey of 1500 managers, together with in-depth case studies of ten organisations in a range of sectors. The findings show that UK managers do regard carbon management as an issue of genuine importance – but that only partial progress has been made.

Almost two-thirds of respondents agreed or strongly agreed that carbon management will become more important in the next three years. The majority of managers (69%) rejected the idea that there is little that their organisation can do to reduce its carbon footprint.

However, only 26% were actively managing their carbon footprint in all their activities, and just one-third of managers had clear measures in place for calculating their carbon footprint. Interestingly, the survey revealed that carbon management practices are more likely to be found in organisations that are growing compared to those that are static or declining. Equally, managers that are 'climate change cynics' – sceptical about carbon management and their ability to reduce their carbon impact – are more likely to work in organisations with low or no growth rates. The group of managers most likely to be climate change cynics is directors.

The findings also showed that larger organisations are more likely to have measures in place for calculating and managing their carbon footprint, and that public sector organisations appear to be taking a strong lead in this area. The top three areas that organisations are targeting to cut carbon dioxide emissions are energy usage in buildings (65%), followed by recycling measures (54%) and fuel usage in transport (45%).

More complex management activities, such as managing carbon dioxide emissions from products and services or along the supply chain, were much less common (14 and 11% respectively).

Case study: EADS Astrium

EADS Astrium is an aerospace, defence and related services operator, with two main sites in the UK and other locations in Germany, France, the Netherlands and Spain. There are approximately 3000 employees in the UK, with 15000 in total across the five countries.

The company's efforts to minimise its environmental impact include minimising travel wherever possible, promoting recycling in all offices on site and using energy-efficient lighting. The organisation has also encouraged car-sharing schemes and has entered a partnership arrangement with a cycling company to persuade employees to bicycle to work. The cycling initiative is further supported by the provision of full shower facilities, proper bike sheds and, in the case of the Stevenage location, an excellent cycle path network.

Two examples of best practice cited by EADS Astrium as part of their environmental strategy include switching their entire lighting to a higher environmental standard and equipping their buildings with transparent rooftops in order to effectively use the daylight. The business has also sought to further reduce lighting costs by recently adding an automatic movement detection system for its offices' fluorescent lighting. Rooms are also equipped with remote control units that enable fluorescent lamps to be turned off completely if not required, or for the lighting to be dimmed on individual lamps. As a result the company has achieved financial savings, particularly in the areas of travel and electricity consumption.

EADS Astrium is also innovating in terms of its products with a view to minimising both costs and disruption to the environment. 'We have increased the service life of a satellite by a factor of three. You put the satellite up and you can now have it working for 15 years, so the manufacturing costs come down.'

The senior management team is highly committed to the organisation's environmental strategy, seeing it as a key means of improving reputation and thereby sustaining the organisation's lead within the sector. Stakeholder feedback has been positive on the organisation's engagement with environmental issues.

The company accepts that there needs to be a long-term understanding of its environmental impact, aside from the actions that can bring quick wins. 'The message we need to get into is ... working on long-term solutions and realising that you're not going to get a return on that work for quite some time. Accept that you're not going to make a profit today, that you've got to wait.'

But this long-term view also goes alongside the 'pursuit of improvement in what we have at the moment', pushing products to their evolutionary limit to get the best from them in terms of their environmental impact.

> (From *Lean and Green: Leadership for the*
> *Low Carbon Economy*, CMI.)

Drivers of green management

The *Lean and Green* research contains some important messages for managers about the issues and behaviours most likely to drive good environmental management practice.

It showed that senior management commitment is the most important driver (cited by 82% of respondents). This is worrying, given the strong scepticism revealed among managers at director level. This group has the responsibility to lead their organisations but the evidence suggests that many are not doing so on this issue. The other significant drivers were cost savings (identified by 78%) and regulation (cited by 75%).

Pressure from existing or potential customers is important or very important for 59 and 62% of managers respectively, while impact on the consumer and employer brand is key for 48 and 42% respectively. Ethical responsibility is regarded as a leading driver by 67%.

The research showed that harnessing employees' commitment and involvement is also vital if environmental management practices are to be driven through successfully. The key is for managers to develop an understanding of employees' personal attitudes about climate change. The research suggested that while the need to cut carbon emissions is widely accepted, differences of opinion exist about why action is necessary. Employees tend to fall into one of four groups. By understanding and appealing to these different groups, managers will be able to target messages appropriately and increase support and involvement.

The four clusters were as follows:

- **Business greens (36%):** Managers that seek to integrate sustainability into their business processes on the basis of the benefits to the business. They are proud of their organisation's environmental performance and have a clear understanding of their environmental impact. Notably, this group was significantly better represented in rapidly growing organisations.
- **Ethical greens (25%):** Managers that are characterised by strong ethical environmental values rather than market- or customer-driven business strategies. They, more than any other group, have a deep personal commitment to climate change issues. They have doubts about the ability of the market to drive low-carbon change and thus view leadership as a crucial driver of environmental innovation. Younger managers and female managers are more likely to fall into one of these first two 'green' groups.

- **Customer-focused greens (21%):** This group was focused primarily on customers and meeting their expectations. As such, they are sensitive to the potential for changes in consumer choices.
- **Non-greens (18%):** This group follow market trends regardless of the environmental impact of their actions and are very sceptical about climate change. Managers in this cluster were particularly predominant among smaller owner-managed or sole trader companies.

To harness employee commitment successfully, managers need to:

- Develop strategies for overcoming resistance to environmental change from different individuals in their organisations, recognising the different sets of motivations that individuals have for responding to the green agenda
- Highlight the multiple and varied benefits of environmental action, including the business benefits, customer engagement, marketing or brand opportunities, as well as the ethical case for action
- Identify champions to lead green initiatives and seek to staff 'green teams' with employees that have supportive personal attitudes
- Include environmental targets or performance bonus arrangements in performance management systems.

It is important to recognise that although engaging employees in environmental initiatives is vital to success, a green approach can also be an important factor in increasing employee engagement. EDF Energy's 2008 Employee Engagement Survey, for example, found sustainability to be the number-one driver of employee engagement within the company.

The CMI's *Lean and Green* survey found that 73% of managers would not want to work for an organisation with a bad environmental reputation. However, substantially fewer (48%) felt pride in the environmental performance of their current employer.

Leader insight

Our values are demonstrated in the way we manage our environmental impact – our products are designed for disassembly and we practice 'reduce, reuse and recycle'. We ensure that spare parts are easily available so that the products have a longer shelf life, and we have an industry-leading low return rate. Those that do make their way back to use are fixed back up and donated to charity or eventually stripped down and recycled. We also designed our new office to have a low carbon footprint. I believe that our environmentally friendly practices have a big emotional impact on our staff and they are a key part of us demonstrating our values.

Rob Law, founder, Magmatic

Taking small steps

In an ideal world all organisations would have a comprehensive strategy for tackling their carbon footprint, carefully thought out and led from the top. An organisational action plan for tackling environmental issues can:

- Provide a coherent statement of policy and a practical system for implementation
- Help to improve communication and management systems by providing information on the carbon footprint of the business
- Lead to more efficient and cost-effective use of resources
- Reduce waste
- Contribute to cost savings and improved productivity
- Lay a foundation for the effective management of environmental risk

- Enhance corporate image by demonstrating to customers, share-holders and the general public that action to reduce damage to the environment is a priority.

This isn't the reality in most organisations, however, and it's important to recognise that even small steps can start to make a difference.

The CMI research highlighted the kinds of practical measures that are most commonly being taken at the moment, as well as those that are likely to be introduced within the next three years. Government could also do more in the public sector, where they have a responsibility as an employer as well as a public policy maker. They could encourage and spread this practice. For example, the NHS has a bigger financial turnover than many developing countries. Demonstrating energy savings in our major hospitals could make a real contribution to reducing the carbon footprint and also give the government added credibility at a time of financial stringency.

The most common green initiative is recycling, which 85% of organisations have introduced, with a further 8% likely to introduce it within the next three years. By comparison, just half (51%) have introduced energy-efficient light bulbs at work, while fewer still have introduced energy-efficient IT. Over the next three years, however, many managers expect to introduce more efficient technologies. Other changes likely to take place will require modifications in business activities, such as more videoconferencing, more remote working and less international travel.

The survey suggests that managers distinguish between factors that are most immediate and directly related to costs – rather than the more abstract measure of carbon emissions. Energy usage and vehicle fuel usage are viewed as very important by 56 and 40% respectively, for example.

Full details are shown in Table 6.1.

Table 6.1 Adoption of measures to reduce energy usage

Measure	Introduced already (%)	To be introduced within 3 years (%)	Would not consider (%)	Don't know (%)
Recycling of waste materials	85	8	2	6
An environmental policy	72	14	3	12
A 'lights out' policy	68	15	4	13
Encourage employees to be more environmentally friendly	64	20	5	12
Energy-efficient light bulbs	51	22	4	23
More remote working	51	23	12	15
Greater use of videoconferencing	51	28	6	16
Greater use of public transport	45	16	17	22
Less international travel	42	18	18	24
Change in product/service specification	36	27	9	28
Energy-efficient IT	33	28	5	34
Changed process policy or process modifications	33	28	7	32
Fuel efficiency measures for car fleet	29	29	9	33
Energy-efficient air conditioning	25	26	9	40
Replacement of high energy-consuming equipment	21	35	8	36
Switching to renewable energy	15	25	11	49

Base: private, N = 316–19; public,: N = 451–4

Of course, managers also have a role to play in encouraging environmental innovation. It is clear that innovation will be necessary if businesses are to achieve changes on the scale needed to meet the challenges posed by climate change.

In particular, there is scope for doing a lot more on waste. The Institution of Mechanical Engineers (IMechE) reports that the UK produces more than 300 million tonnes of waste per year, which is enough to fill the Albert Hall every two years. In its report *A Wasted Opportunity*, the IMechE advocates that waste should not be regarded as a problem to be 'dealt with', but as a valuable resource that could help create new and sustainable sources of energy and reduce the need for landfill.

There is a view that the government should stimulate innovation by incentivising companies to continually look for long-term sustainable solutions. This is an area of policy that has not yet been addressed and there are still no tools or measures in place to guide managers through this approach. Managers can, however, make sure that they consider environmental impact in all product, service or process innovation. It is particularly important for leaders to show commitment to this approach and to reward managers for appropriate behaviours. We talk more about the role of managers in stimulating innovation in Chapter 7.

Case study: Royal Mail

Royal Mail operates primarily in the postal sector but is also in logistics and communication. It employs 165 000 staff across the UK, with 33 000 vehicles operating across 3000 sites.

Royal Mail has had a carbon management strategy in place for several years, with a programme of activity looking at how it can reduce its carbon consumption effectively over periods of five to ten years. Given the nature of the business, the main areas of focus are on fuel and transport, alongside energy use, particularly in buildings. Additional sustainability targets on waste, landfill and water consumption feature prominently in the strategy.

Royal Mail is clear on its commitment to a series of targets, including reducing its total carbon dioxide transport emissions by 20% by 2010, reducing the solid waste it sends to landfill by 25%, reducing fresh water consumption by 5% and reducing greenhouse gas emissions from building energy use by 10%. It has an overall stretch target of reducing total carbon dioxide emissions by 50% by 2015.

The corporate social responsibility (CSR) team determined the organisation's environmental objectives and is responsible for both developing and implementing the carbon management programme. Development of these objectives was carried out in conjunction with the Carbon Trust.

A CSR committee made up of managing directors across Royal Mail Group's brands and chaired by the chief executive leads implementation of the strategy. This council provides high-level visibility across the organisation and approval at this senior level helps to remove obstacles further down the organisational chain.

Royal Mail is working towards developing formal internal networks with local champions to support the business in driving through change. Additionally, there is increased emphasis on creating accountability by looking at how environmental aspects can be built into business targets for senior managers. Environmental aspects are also incorporated into all business case submissions, so that there is a 'green consideration' in everything the organisation does.

A carbon management board, with representation from senior leaders covering each of the directorates, was set up to ensure that sustainability targets were embedded and monitored, and as a means to avoid any barriers to implementation. The organisation is conscious of the need to deliver better communications to help drive employee engagement.

One of the most effective initiatives in the organisation's carbon management strategy has been the transport review, which looked to model different ways to run the fleet of vehicles. Following remodelling, the Royal Mail was able to reduce its overall carbon footprint by approximately 120000 tons per year. Other initiatives include looking at training staff to drive in a more environmentally friendly way and rewarding customers for producing 'sustainable mailings' that reduce waste through better targeting and are easy to recycle.

Royal Mail is ranked third in the International Post Corporation's assessment of carbon management programmes in postal organisations around the world. This not only demonstrates the achievements of the organisation, but has also led to shared understanding of best practice across the sector.

Royal Mail views a highly successful carbon management programme as integral to its future and to capitalising on potential new commercial opportunities. In terms of the present economic climate, the organisation accepts that it will have to get 'very creative' at how it delivers carbon reduction.

(From *Lean and Green: Leadership for the Low Carbon Economy*, CMI.)

Getting to grips with regulation

As the pressure to meet stretching environmental targets intensifies, it will become increasingly important for managers to get to grips with regulations in this field. Feedback from the survey suggests this is an area that many executives struggle with, either because of lack of in-house resources or due to the complexity of the relevant rules.

In addition to meeting their regulatory obligations, there are opportunities for companies to go for accreditation and verification. The most widespread relevant standard is ISO 14001, which was being used by one in five survey respondents (www.iso.org). A smaller number were following the Carbon Accounting Guidelines (PAS 2050), which can be used to improve and report on the greenhouse gas performance of products and services.

Work needs to be done to communicate the potential usefulness of these and other measures and standards. The CMI survey suggests that around 46% of respondents take a positive view of regulation and believe that it helps to drive higher standards of environmental practice, encourage innovation and create new markets. A larger group of 54%, however, perceive regulation as a barrier towards achieving their strategic goals and believe it can lead to an expensive, bureaucratic tick-box compliance culture.

Managers need to make sure they develop a clear understanding of the practicalities and benefits of regulation so that they can communicate and demonstrate the advantages to their teams. As much as possible, these green teams should straddle departments and hierarchies, involving younger managers who have a strong personal commitment to the environment.

Future challenges

The biggest challenge facing managers is to move away from the 'low-hanging fruit' such as waste management and recycling to more radical service, product or manufacturing change.

This will, however, require incentivisation and clear leadership. Unless there are clear signals coming from the top, commitment will waver and may even die. At a time when we have to make difficult choices about use of management time, it is tempting to downplay the role of managing the carbon footprint or respecting the environment. This is not, however, an issue that can be put on the back burner. Businesses need to start establishing 'green teams' that can monitor environmental performance, look for changes that can be implemented in both the short and long term, and report on progress.

There are plenty of opportunities for businesses to learn from each other, too. There is a host of support and information bodies who can help spread best practice – including the CMI, which can facilitate networking and provide access to the latest information.

We also need to move towards a situation where environmental performance is included in an organisation's key performance indicators (KPIs), scrutinised when businesses are choosing which suppliers to contract with and covered in detail in the company report and accounts.

Checklist: Taking action on the environment

- **Gain the commitment of senior management:** Make sure the implications of good and bad environmental practice are fully understood by top managers and key stakeholders. Responsibility for environmental matters should be allocated at senior level in order to ensure that effective action is taken.
- **Identify environmental laws and regulations:** Do your homework on relevant legislation and codes of practice, and check which regulations apply to businesses in your sector or specialist field. Bear in mind that failure to comply with regulations may incur financial penalties. The websites of Defra and the Environment Agency provide useful starting points for research.
- **Consider whether to apply for registration under ISO 14001 or EMAS:** Registration provides a recognised framework for environmental management and may contribute to competitive advantage.
- **Review the environmental impact of your organisation's operations:** Cover all aspects of the business from systems to staff, and all stages of the product of service life cycle. Factors to be

taken into account include energy use, waste management, transportation and procurement, as well as more obvious issues such as emissions of greenhouse gases and other pollutants. Monitoring changes in the external environment will also help you to identify issues that need to be addressed and improvements that need to be made, and to be aware of threats and opportunities for the future.

- **Work out the environment-business link:** This will help you to make the business case for sustainability and environmentally friendly policies. Focus on issues where environmental improvements can be directly related to financial and quality targets; for example, generating new raw materials through recycling waste, or the rationalisation of price increases for more eco-friendly products.

- **Establish your policy:** Draw up a clear statement covering objectives, improvement programmes, audits, supplier and customer liaison, compliance with standards, and responsibility to the community.

- **Build in measures and records:** These should cover not only outputs (damage to, or impact on, the environment) and inputs (damage created by raw materials), but also process measures (pollution created by out-of-date or worn-out machinery). Keep detailed records – legislation and ISO 14001 may require evidence of compliance.

- **Develop a procedures manual:** The manual should be a 'who does what and how' of operational control, achieved through work instructions, performance indicators, measurements, tests and verification.

- **Launch an environmental training programme:** Build environmental protection and sustainability into routine operational practice. The organisation will benefit from environmental goals being integrated with financial, operational and personal targets.

- **Involve your employees:** Consult with and involve your employees at every stage of the process. Raising levels of eco-awareness and communicating the benefits within the organisation will help gain commitment to environmentally friendly policies and practices. Publicise the objectives and targets that have been set.

- **Consider the development of partnerships with stakeholders:** Working with shareholders, suppliers and local communities can be an effective way to develop innovative and creative ways to enhance environmental performance.

- **Conduct regular audits:** Systematic gathering of information to monitor the effectiveness of environmental policies now often forms part of an organisation's total environmental management system. It is concerned with checking compliance with legislative requirements and environmental standards, as well as with company policy. Use audits to monitor the effectiveness of the policy, correct what is going wrong and publicise what is going right.

- **Communicate environmental benefits internally and externally:** Environmental reporting is becoming more widespread and will reap benefits in terms of public image and reputation. Amendments to the Companies Act 1985 required the inclusion of information on environmental performance in the annual business review. Defra has produced guidelines designed to facilitate the process that include 22 KPIs. The impact of improvements in environmental performance should be expressed in financial terms where possible, but also in terms of direct benefits to the community.

Key questions

- Are you demonstrating personal commitment to the environmental agenda and communicating a clear sense of direction?
- Do you have measures in place to help build engagement across the organisation (e.g. green teams)?
- Does the organisation have environment-related targets included in the performance management systems for individual managers, helping to drive change throughout the company?
- Are you drawing on the enthusiasm of younger managers who are passionate about the agenda to help push through change?
- Are you properly informed about how carbon emissions are measured and managed so that you can calculate your carbon footprint?
- Have you embedded sustainability and low carbon objectives in procurement processes?
- Have you clearly identified the saving you could make as a company from a variety of energy saving schemes, e.g. waste reduction, recycling, transport to work schemes, working from home, etc? Have you understood and analysed other companies' best practices?
- Is your low-carbon vision communicated consistently both externally and internally, e.g. in brand and marketing messages, in new staff induction, and in training for existing staff?

In this chapter we have looked at how tackling green issues can add real value to the bottom line and have shared some of the latest thinking on how organisations can become 'leaner and greener'. As you have read, managing green concerns effectively can create enormous potential for innovation. In Chapter 7 we go on to look at how managers can encourage innovation within their teams and ensure that new and exciting ideas come to fruition.

CHAPTER 7

If you find it difficult to accept failure then you simply won't get any innovation, because employees will be too frightened.

Sir Terry Leahy, CEO, Tesco, quoted in
Professional Manager, January 2010

UK plc has a mixed track record when it comes to innovation. We have a wealth of scientific expertise and know-how; the number of graduates becoming qualified in key science, technology, engineering and mathematics skills continues to rise; and the UK remains in the top five on the EU's 'scoreboard' for innovation performance. However, only one in five managers has any qualification for the job they do.

When it comes to putting great ideas into practice, however, the UK is still lagging behind many of its competitors. Business investment in research and development (R&D) remains low overall, with private equity and venture capital in particular taking a nosedive over the past two years.

The recession has, of course, played a part in this downturn in funding, but in a difficult economic climate, organisations need to innovate more than ever before. Increasing global competition means that it's no longer enough for businesses to compete on price alone. They need to come up with new and exciting ideas that will help them stand out from the crowd and attract new customers. Public sector organisations, faced with swingeing cuts, also need to find ways to break the mould and come up with alternative and creative ways of delivering front-line services.

Leaders and managers have a vital role to play in creating the conditions where innovation can flourish. There needs to be a clear message from the very top of the organisation that innovation is valued and will be encouraged and rewarded. Leaders such as Lord Bilimoria, founder of Cobra Beer, and Rita Clifton, past CEO and now Chair of Interbrand, are prime examples of how innovation can be driven from the top.

Managers on the front line need to encourage cultures where off-the-wall thinking is encouraged and new ideas are not dismissed out of hand. They need to find ways of overcoming some of the barriers to innovation and ensuring that the new ideas and thinking generated by their team get beyond the drawing board.

In this chapter we look at the process of innovation, explore the challenges and opportunities presented by the recession, and share some of the latest research on how organisations can successfully drive innovative approaches. We also give advice on the practical steps managers can take to encourage innovation in their teams and describe how some of the UK's top leaders approach this task themselves.

Innovation in practice

Mention the word 'innovation' and the image that springs to mind is of IT geeks hunched over their computers in pursuit of the next technological advance, or white-coated scientists working late in the lab.

But innovation isn't just about ground-breaking new products or world shattering scientific discoveries – although these are what tend to hit the headlines. Often it is the small incremental changes to products, services or processes that can put organisations ahead of their competitors.

Put simply, innovation is the successful exploitation of ideas. For one organisation, it might mean developing a new product or service that catches the public imagination or meets a pressing consumer need. For another, design of a new manufacturing process might lead to faster delivery times and more competitive pricing.

In the public sector, innovation can come in the shape of a new management approach that results in more efficient use of resources – or it might mean a leading edge initiative to join forces with a private or voluntary sector partner to deliver a critical service in a new way.

A whole host of different factors serve to stimulate innovation. Often it's driven by developments in technology, pressure to cut costs or the search to find more efficient ways of tackling business issues. Sometimes exciting advances come about simply because of human curiosity and an innate desire to keep searching for new and different ways of doing things. We certainly seem to have an infinite capacity to create wants and needs, developing new products that have functionality we never knew we needed.

Take the mobile phone, for example. As recently as the early 1990s, it was a rarity and targeted mainly at City types who needed to keep in touch while on the move. Now everyone, from your children to your granny, regards it as an essential item, and it has revolutionised the way we conduct our business and social lives. It connects us to a world of information 24/7, allows us to conduct business any time and from anywhere, and gives us the ability to keep in constant touch with friends and family, wherever they might be.

From small beginnings, the mobile phone business has become enormous and now contributes £15 billion a year to the UK's GDP. Today there are more than 80 million mobile connections in the UK, which were used to send more than 100 billion text messages last year. Development continues apace, with more than 12 million people now owning a smartphone, which allows them to access Internet and web-based services.

There are also many examples from history of how innovations can have major spin-offs that are not even dreamed of at the time. When President John F. Kennedy committed the US to putting the first man on the moon, thus starting the space race, he could not have known that a by-product of the enormous surge in scientific and technological knowledge would be the capacity to feed the planet. When the Industrial Revolution took place in 19th century Britain, the discovery of steam power not only revolutionised the transport industry but also opened up vast markets for its products as the growth of railways spread across the Empire.

These examples illustrate that innovation can spread very quickly, but it's important to recognise that it can also be snuffed out. It will only thrive if organisations, and the financial institutions that support them, are prepared to invest, take risks and dedicate time, resources and imagination to finding new ways of tackling old problems.

We need much more collaboration and cross-fertilisation across industry and education in the UK if we are to raise our game. The US economy, for example, has been much better at aligning the academic knowledge base with the needs of industry. There are now technology clusters across the US where academics, entrepreneurs and innovators work closely together refining ideas, proving concepts and commercialising the fruits of their labour.

This is happening in the UK too, in the Oxford and Cambridge science parks and at universities such as Liverpool, Loughborough, Warwick and Birmingham, where the science and engineering communities are developing close links with local industries and working on projects for national and multinational companies.

Organisations need to be much more proactive on this front, seeking out partners who can help them develop the new insights that will drive their business forward. It's a mistake, however, to think that innovation is an activity that belongs solely in the R&D department and is reserved for specialists and technicians. Innovation can't be put in a box – and sometimes it comes from the most unlikely corners of the organisation. It's about people, and giving them the skills to succeed, the permission to experiment and reward for their efforts.

The National Society for the Prevention of Cruelty to Children (NSPCC), for example, developed secondment/staff development opportunities as a way of supplementing the training and development budget. These opportunities were created by corporate donors. Not only did it eke out the budget, it also allowed the NSPCC to generate additional commitment from its donors, who actually gained far more from being involved as business coaches and mentors than they had previously from just contributing funds.

Case study: Innovation at Saint-Gobain British Gypsum

Innovation and innovative working are a key part of the drive to create sustainable competitive advantage at Saint-Gobain British Gypsum, the UK's leading manufacturer of plasterboard and plaster-based systems and products.

HR Director Richard Batley explains that when the company's vision was being developed, the senior team recognised that clear communication about innovation was going to be vital:

> We had to articulate what innovative working looks like in our organisation. We had to define it for people and we were keen not to set off in delivering lots of initiatives. When we said innovation was in the vision we had some doubts expressed, but we were persistent and kept on with the message to the point that people eventually did understand it and support it. We encouraged a tolerance for novelty, raised awareness of our customers' needs for change and began using a process of customer insight to drive innovation.

To signal change and start to move organisational behaviour, the company deliberately used innovation language in the Technical Director's job title and made specific and regular references in meeting agendas and internal communications. It also appointed a senior manager, whose title was Innovation Manager, and introduced an 'Innov8' ideas scheme.

The executive team also thought deeply about how they could combine culture and behaviour with the process disciplines that sit behind innovation. A decision was made to bring the HR and technical functions together to facilitate the changes.

The push to promote innovative working was underpinned by a strong emphasis on appropriate skills training and development. Project leadership training was developed to bring cross-functional teams together effectively, for example.

'The amount of resource we have spent on training and skills development directly correlates with our product development outputs,' says Jan Rideout, Innovation Technical Director, who continues:

> We also improved the quality of feedback and recognition that our people received through the appraisal system. The Executive were committed to ensuring everyone in the business had regular feedback, that excellent performance is rewarded and employees were presented with stretching but realistic targets. We made sure we celebrated good work rather than creating a 'bad news' climate. It was challenging at first, especially in communicating what innovation looks like in terms of behaviours. The execs were also keen to see early pay-offs and I had to fight my corner in reinforcing the message that innovation takes time. Our focus was on everyday innovation more than radical, revolutionary innovation.

HR Director Richard Batley says that the business has seen its ability to hit project milestones almost double over the last two years as a result of its focus on innovation. 'We are encouraging people to think differently, work cross-functionally and in networks,' he says. 'Organisations label people functionally, and I think this can be a real barrier to using skills and knowledge available to drive innovation and change.'

(From *Everyday Innovation: How to Enhance Innovative Working in Employees and Organisations*, published by Nesta, www.nesta.org.uk.)

Barriers to innovation

Research conducted recently by the CMI and Nesta (the National Endowment for Science, Technology and the Arts) highlights some of the attitudes and practices that are holding us back when it comes to innovation.

The report *Innovation for the Recovery: Enhancing Innovative Working Practices* presented the findings from a survey of CMI members carried out at the height of the recession. The results show that the top three barriers to innovation are financial constraints (cited by almost half of respondents), lack of time and lack of resources. These top three 'blockers' were universal across sectors.

Other barriers highlighted included risk aversion, unclear leadership and lack of autonomy. Managers reported that lack of talent, insufficient incentives and inadequate training also had a tendency to get in the way. A blame culture was also perceived to be a key barrier, particularly by those working in the public sector. Full details are shown in Table 7.1.

Table 7.1 Barriers to innovative working

Barrier	Respondents saying the barrier is significant (%)
Excessive financial constraints	49
Lack of time	46
Lack of resources	36
Risk aversion and a fear of failure among leaders	28
An overly hierarchical structure across staff levels	25
Unclear leadership strategy and goals towards innovation	22
Insufficient incentives in place to encourage innovation	18
Insufficient training and development resources for innovative ideas	18
Insufficient talent for innovation	16
A lack of autonomy in job roles	14
Insufficient opportunities and mechanisms to share knowledge with others	14

There were some interesting differences in perceived barriers to innovation between managers working in larger and smaller organisations. Managers in large organisations were more likely to report a lack of incentives to encourage innovation, while smaller organisations more often struggled with having insufficient talent for innovation. Leaders and managers need to find ways to overcome these obstacles by developing strategies and approaches that allow innovation to flourish.

Impact of the recession

The recession has clearly had an impact on both the desire and ability of organisations to innovate. Two-thirds of managers in the CMI/Nesta survey said their organisation's approach to innovation was likely to change as a result of the economic situation, with the majority (58%) agreeing that it had already changed over the previous year.

Many managers also said that the level of importance given to innovation in their personal job role had declined because of the economy. Only one-third reported that innovation was among the individual goals that had been set for them.

There was a definite contrast between the way large and small organisations viewed the downturn and its likely impact on innovation. Managers in large organisations were more likely to agree that resources for innovation would be reduced and that the percentage of workforce time dedicated to it would decrease. Managers in small organisations, however, felt that individuals would be given more freedom and opportunities to innovate. They felt that in difficult economic times, team members would be more cooperative and willing to combine their efforts.

It is understandable that at a time when everything is uncertain and budgets are under intense pressure, managers have a tendency to focus on survival rather than growth. But innovation can't be put on the 'for later' pile. In the current economic climate it's not only critical to success, it's often a prerequisite for survival.

Organisations need to find ways of responding quickly to challenges, adopting new ideas and moving fast to seize opportunities. Previous experience suggests that the context of a recession can in fact provide a strong stimulus for innovation and growth.

The economist Joseph Schumpeter wrote in the 1940s about the importance of 'creative destruction', arguing that economic change, however difficult and disruptive, is often associated with technological and procedural progress and transformation. As we look to build a sustainable recovery from this recession, managers need to stop 'fire fighting' and think strategically about how they can unlock the innovative potential of their organisations.

Leader insights

Now more than ever, there is an imperative to innovate ... The priorities within innovation have changed, with organisations showing a greater focus on delivery of returns.
Jon Bentley, Innovation Leader, IBM Global Business Services
(quoted in Nesta report)

The economic crisis should be used as a catalyst for innovation. If that opportunity is not taken, the long-term costs can be even greater.
Claire Whitaker, Director at international music producer Serious
(quoted in Nesta report)

Innovation in the public sector

Managers in the public sector face even more of an uphill struggle when it comes to encouraging innovation.

The CMI/Nesta research suggests that public sector organisations are less well equipped to promote and facilitate new thinking and ideas. The survey found fewer working practices conducive to innovation and more managerial barriers.

There is widespread concern that spending cuts will make the situation worse. Public sector managers were more likely than their private sector counterparts to feel that the resources available for innovation will be reduced as belts tighten. Fear of failure among public sector leaders was highlighted as one of the key blockers to innovation, together with hierarchical and bureaucratic organisation structures.

Innovation is also a key performance goal for fewer employees in the public sector. Only 13% said their organisation had a high percentage of employees with such goals, compared to 28% in the private sector.

Table 7.2 compares the responses of private and public sector employees.

Table 7.2 Innovative working practices significantly more prevalent in the private sector than the public ($p < 0.05$)

Working practice	Private sector agreement (%)	Public sector agreement (%)
We strive for a reputation for being innovative	74	63
The general management style is participative and supportive	73	60
There is a 'no blame' culture – mistakes are talked about freely so others can learn from them	60	44
Resources and facilities are readily available for use in testing out new ideas	54	36
Job assignments ensure that there is enough time and scope for trying out new ideas	40	29
The appraisal system is directly linked to rewarding creativity and innovation	34	29

There is no doubt that managers in the public sector are under unprecedented pressure to achieve more with less, but this is no time to put innovation on the back burner. Leaders need to actively encourage new and creative approaches, and to ensure that innovation is not being stifled in their teams.

Leader insight

We really need transformation to be happening in the public sector and that means taking risks, but that's hard when your failures might end up on the front of the newspaper.

Penny de Valk, Chief Executive Officer, Institute of Leadership and Management (ILM)

Facilitating innovation

The key to maximising innovation is to unleash the knowledge, skills and abilities of employees. This is a core task for managers. By adopting the right working practices, building and leading the right teams, and providing the necessary resources, managers play a crucial role in making sure that their organisation finds the 'silver bullets' that will give it the edge.

Managers recognise they have an important role to play in encouraging innovation. Eighty per cent of those taking part in the CMI/Nesta survey agreed or strongly agreed with the statement 'Innovation is an important part of my job role'.

The research clearly identified the practices and behaviours that act as catalysts for innovation within organisations. The first and most crucial factor is that managers have an open and supportive approach to innovation (identified by 46% of respondents). The second most highly rated factor was for leaders to model behaviours that encourage innovation (40%), while around a third (32%) identified setting up the right team of people as critical.

Managers in the private sector cited flat organisational structures as a top catalyst for innovation. Incentive and reward programmes that encouraged innovative behaviours were also key.

One particularly interesting difference emerged in the not-for-profit sector: managers were more likely to cite tolerance of failure and promotion of risk-taking (34%) as a catalyst for innovation than managers in the private sector (19%).

The most popular catalysts for innovation are shown in Table 7.3.

Table 7.3 Top catalysts for innovation

Catalyst	Respondents working for organisations that have these catalysts (%)
Managers' support and openness to innovation	46
Leaders modelling behaviours that encourage innovation	40
Setting up the right team of people for innovation efforts	32
Autonomy and freedom in carrying out job roles	29
Senior leadership's development of an innovation strategy and related priorities	26
Tolerance of failure and promotion of risk-taking	23
Development of networking opportunities	19
Dedicated resources for innovative ideas and development	18
Incentives or reward programmes that encourage innovation	18
Clear targets and metrics for innovation initiatives	15
Investment in talent for innovation	14
A flat organisational structure	14

Case study: Cobra Beer

(Lord Karan Bilimoria is founder and chairman of Cobra Beer and one of the UK's best-known entrepreneurs. In his book *Against the Grain* he describes how the business creates an environment where innovation can flourish.)

'At Cobra Beer it means keeping an open atmosphere in our office where there are few rules, and where people from all parts of the company are encouraged to come up with ideas.

'You can have mechanisms that encourage this. For a time, for example, we ran an 'idea of the month' scheme. An empty box of Cobra served as an ideas box, and everyone from the company was encouraged to put in ideas over the course of the month. Then one volunteer from the company would go through the ideas and select the best three from the month, which in turn would be recognised, acknowledged and rewarded. Most importantly, they were put into action.

'These ideas might be a marketing idea that had been put forward by somebody in the accounts department, or an idea to do with draught beer that was suggested by somebody in marketing – something you would have expected a salesperson to come up with. Then there must be a follow-up scheme where somebody makes sure that the ideas are implemented.

'An important part of this process is not just the aspect of generating ideas, but making everyone in the company feel part of the overall business – the overall brand – and not just part of their particular speciality. This promotes integration and cross-silo working and breaks down barriers. It is a virtuous circle, because the more open the environment, the more innovation there is. Although Cobra now has a dedicated innovation team

*and a streamlined, professional innovation process, it was in that
early "idea of the month" scheme where the seed of innovation
was planted.'*

Lord Bilimoria's essential ingredients for innovation
A spirit of restless innovation is essential for success:

- Aspire to create an organisational culture where innovation can thrive.
- Try to keep rules to a minimum; encourage everyone to pitch in with ideas, no matter how leftfield; recognise and reward the best contributions.
- Innovation is not just 'ideas' – follow up and make sure that the good ideas are implemented.
- Create a dedicated innovation team.
- Build your brand's heritage.
- Learn to think the unthinkable. Use techniques like brainstorming to help.

(From *Against the Grain: Lessons in Entrepreneurship from
the Founder of Cobra Beer*, Capstone, 2009.)

Leader insights

*Leaders play a crucial role in fostering innovation; they must provide
employees with the right mandate and provide autonomy within a given
framework.*

Derek Smith, CEO, UBS Poland Service Centre
(quoted in Nesta report)

> *Managers of innovative groups, those of high-performing teams, act as a shield – taking the flak. Symbolically, this signals to the team they are safe to do what they need to do.*
>
> Linda Holbeche, former Director of Research and Policy, CIPD (quoted in Nesta report)

> *Employees' annual appraisals and quarterly performance reviews are aligned with innovation, one of the organisation's core values. It really does work.*
>
> Brett Terry, Head of HR and Organisational Development, UK breast cancer charity Breakthrough (quoted in Nesta report)

Case study: Innovative working at Amey

Amey is one of the country's leading public services providers, helping to manage the UK's infrastructure and business services, including motorways, public transport, local schools and council services. It has a team of 11 000 employees spread across the UK.

The business has a formal innovation agenda led by its Business Improvement Team (BIT), members of which are 'parachuted' into different projects as and when needed. Amey also has innovation forums and 'champions' within each of its contract groups.

The business seeks, however, to make innovation an integral part of how employees outside of these specialist teams approach their work. 'Many people have a reaction to the word "innovation", either thinking it's not what they do or it is done elsewhere in the company,' says Scott Hobbs, Head of Talent. 'Although we want the blue sky thinkers, we can't sustain this and what we really need is everyday innovation. We are seeking people able to take innovation and process it in practical terms.'

In looking for the appropriate behaviours to support innovation, Amey's approach has been to focus on the talent it already has – as well as on new recruits coming into the business. An integral part of the talent pipeline is ensuring that behaviours and values that support innovation are embedded in the system of graduate selection and development. Currently, the graduate programme takes on 125 recruits per year in areas such as engineering. Assessment centres for graduates use exercises that test elements of innovative and creative thinking, as well as the implementation of new ideas (e.g. ways of marketing particular products).

The business underlines its view that innovation is part of the 'day job' by not making specific financial rewards for innovative working, although it does have a best practice forum that provides a mechanism for recognition of ideas. 'The view on rewards and innovation is that the company policy should be directed to free people up to take part in innovative activities/practice. Reward is not necessary as activities relating to innovation are part of their job,' says Hobbs.

(From *Everyday Innovation: How to Enhance Innovative Working in Employees and Organisations*, Nesta, www.nesta.org.uk.)

 Checklist: Creating an innovation friendly culture

- **Developing your personal style:** Do you truly believe in the value of innovation? Do you have the energy to drive changes through and make them happen? Can you cope with the ambiguity and uncertainty necessary to manage innovation successfully? Are your facilitation, problem-solving and risk management skills up to scratch? The Department of Business, Innovation & Skills' website (www.bis.gov.uk) has a useful tool that can help you decide whether you are innovation proactive, neutral or agnostic.

There is also a self-assessment tool to help you gauge how well you are managing the process of innovation in your team.

- **Creating the right culture:** Are you creating a culture where people feel safe to experiment with new ideas and step outside of their normal boundaries? If people think they will be shouted down, they won't speak up when they have a new idea. Make sure the underlying culture is not suffocating innovative ideas before they reach the surface.

- **Recognising innovative employees:** Who are the innovative people in your team? Would you know how to recognise them? The top characteristics of innovative employees are openness to ideas, problem-solving skills and personal initiative/motivation. Innovative people are also typically strong in strategic thinking, self-confidence/belief, willingness to take risks, emotional intelligence and ability to cope with change and uncertainty.

- **Supporting innovative employees:** How well are you supporting your employees in their attempts to break new ground? Innovative people need help and support from their manager when it comes to putting their ideas into practice. They need someone to keep them motivated when the going gets tough and to help them plan and organise the steps they need to take to bring their ideas to fruition.

- **Breaking down barriers:** Make sure you are not being political and parochial with the innovative ideas that emerge from your team. Sometimes managers are reluctant to share ideas that have been developed by their people with the rest of the business, because they perceive they will lose power and kudos. Equally, they can be defensive about adopting new ideas that have been developed elsewhere. Innovation needs to be shared so that its full potential can be realised.

- **Taking risks:** Risk and innovation go hand in hand. Not all good ideas are perfect to begin with – there may be flaws that need to be ironed out and issues that need to be resolved. Managing innovation successfully means welcoming new ideas, accepting they may not hit the mark first time round and being prepared to accept failure. Innovative employees need to know they have a senior champion who will speak up and support them if or when things go pear-shaped.

- **Encouraging innovation:** Innovation will only happen if managers devote sufficient time and resources to it, and allow their employees to do the same. People need time and space to sit back and think and talk about new ideas. Other initiatives that can help to encourage innovation include setting up cross-functional teams, holding brainstorming sessions or organising job secondments. Leadership and management training can also help to stimulate new thinking and approaches.

- **Rewarding innovation:** Are you rewarding people who demonstrate the kind of innovative behaviour you want to encourage? Think about how you are incentivising your team and recognising and celebrating their successes. Research has found that team incentives are often more successful than individual reward, emphasising the important role having the right team plays in pushing innovation forward.

- **Encouraging networking:** It's a good idea to encourage people to step outside of their usual environment and connect with others. They can get closer to customers, for example, so they can get a better understanding of the issues that the customers are facing and how, as a supplier, you might be able to offer something better. Encourage internal networking too. Try and act like a broker, bringing people from different departments together so they can create new thinking and generate innovative ideas.

In this chapter we have looked at what managers need to do to stimulate innovation and ensure that new ideas are not unwittingly stifled. As you have read, there is enormous potential for organisations to make an innovative approach a key part of their corporate brand. In Chapter 8 we go on to look at the role that managers need to play in building, maintaining and enhancing their organisation's brand and reputation.

CHAPTER 8

Great brands are based on authenticity and trust. Ethics and values are critical. Organisations who say one thing and do another risk suicide.
Rita Clifton, UK Chairman, Interbrand

When times are tough, the strength and durability of an organisation's brand and reputation can be the difference between sinking or swimming.

Take Marks & Spencer, for example. The business has been through some tumultuous times in recent years, but has managed to stand firm because customers know and respect the quality, value and service ethos it stands for.

Apple is another example of an organisation that is successfully using its brand to stay a step ahead of the competition. The technology behind its products is universal, but thanks to the brand values it holds dear – innovation and staying one step ahead – its products are widely regarded as the latest 'must have'.

Brand value can take years to build. But as many organisations have found to their cost, it can also very quickly be undermined. A breakdown in the supply chain, a failure to communicate, a whiff of industrial unrest – all these can undermine consumer confidence and turn into a PR disaster almost overnight.

This makes it vital for organisations to have management processes in place that support the brand and ensure its potential is exploited to the full. Managers also have a vital role to play in making sure employees buy into the brand and reflect the brand values on a day-to-day basis in their work.

Branding has always been seen as the preserve of the marketing department – and it is of course quite right that they should remain in control and behind the steering wheel. Managers could, however, benefit from developing a more sophisticated understanding of marketing principles.

In their recent book *War in the Boardroom*, Al and Laura Ries argue that the 'velvet curtain' separating marketing people from management people needs to be torn down. The gulf between the disciplines is too wide and people often make management decisions without fully understanding the marketing consequences. They point out, for example, that managers deal in reality (facts and figures) while marketing people deal in perceptions (what's actually in the mind of consumers). This means that management focus is often on cutting costs and improving processes, rather than on investing in activities that build brands and help to ensure a sustainable future for the business.

This chapter looks at the manager's role in supporting the brand and protecting corporate reputation. It provides practical guidance on how managers can encourage employees to 'live the brand', how they can engage stakeholders in supporting the brand and on the importance of measuring brand equity.

Exploiting the brand

It is surprising how many businesses fail to fully exploit their brand. Strong brands have generally been hard won, and leaders and managers need to make sure they are taking pride in the reputation of their company and its products and services.

They need to have their antennae constantly tuned for opportunities to build further on their strengths – and to sense when the brand may be under threat from new competitors or changes in the market.

Managers who want to support successful, ongoing exploitation of their brand need to ask themselves the following questions:

- Where do the real strengths of the business lie? What is the core of its expertise and what is it really good at?
- How can the business reinforce its assets by doing more of the things it excels at? Where does it need to focus its future efforts?
- How well is the company communicating its brand values? Is it conveying the message about what the brand stands for effectively to both employees and the outside world?
- Is the business doing enough to generate a sense of pride about the brand by shouting about its successes to employees, stakeholders, partners and customers/clients?
- Is the business adequately investing in the brand for the future? Has sufficient budget been allocated to activities that will help to reinforce the brand?

The virtual disappearance of 'Brand Britain' over recent years is a prime example of what can happen when organisations fail to ask themselves these questions. As a result of numerous corporate mergers and takeovers, we have lost many of the long-established brands that were synonymous with Britain. As economic conditions continue to be challenging, others are under threat.

There is, however, still plenty of potential for the UK to proactively build on its strengths. There is enormous potential, for example, for growth in the arts and media, where the country already has an outstanding record for creativity. The film industry in particular is going through a revival, with companies such as Warner Bros. investing in major production facilities in the UK. The Olympics will also provide an opportunity for 'Team GB' to showcase its leading edge in the field of both sport and the arts.

Higher education is another area where the UK has an outstanding reputation. Qualifications in areas such as accountancy, engineering and human resource management are respected and sought after around the world. As global barriers break down, this is a position that could be further exploited in order to retain competitive advantage.

When considering how to best exploit the brand, managers also need to recognise that brands and reputations are both corporate and individual. The actions and inactions of organisations and individuals can have a significant effect on the brand. If too much is vested in the individual brand, the organisation can suffer. This is why organisational brands need to be durable and built to last.

Leader insights

This is a very creative nation on an individual basis; we need to scale up to make things happen collectively, leaving our half-empty glass at home where it belongs.
    Kai Peters, Chief Executive, Ashridge Business School, quoted in
                                                        Management Today

The Serious Fraud Office has a very strong and trusted brand. This is sacrosanct. We are also very clear about what we stand for.
        Phillippa Williamson, Chief Executive, Serious Fraud Office

Land Rover, Jaguar and Rolls-Royce are long-lasting British brands because they stand for quality and integrity. They have earned a reputation for being trustworthy.
    David Noble, Chief Executive, Chartered Institute of Purchasing
                                                    and Supply (CIPS)

Case study: Fortnum & Mason

Fortnum & Mason is an example of a retail organisation that has increased its business by successful exploitation of its quintessentially 'British' brand. The iconic store, known as the Queen's grocer, has recently completed a refurbishment – as a result of which it has turned in the best profits for a decade.

Under the direction of MD Beverley Aspinall, the store has also focused its offering around the four core areas where it had an existing strong reputation. Out went whole departments such as ladies' fashion and hairdressing, to concentrate on food, wine, entertaining and gifts – the areas that Fortnum & Mason was best known for.

The food hall was rearranged, with new fresh meat and fish counters being introduced, together with dedicated areas for cheese, a bakery and a deli. This meant the store could give more space to its core lines such as tea, preserves, biscuits, cakes and confectionery, all of which have been trading incredibly well. There's also a new cookshop and a wine bar to complete the store's existing restaurants, which include the very British St James'.

Aspinall is in no doubt that Fortnum's USP is its brand; a brand moreover with countless historic highlights such as when Queen Victoria ordered dried soup to be sent to Florence Nightingale for the troops in Crimea.

'Our brand is hugely important. It gives us a global reach,' she says. 'It is synonymous with Englishness. Fortnum buyers scour the country for the very best – mainly artisan producers at the top end of the quality scale.' Buyers themselves often come up with ideas for new products – especially food – with input into the packaging and placement.

Visitors find the elegant Fortnum's logo on boxes, bows, labels and lids, from Bah Humbugs in gorgeous jars to embossed biscuit tubes. It is a triumph of marrying taste to design. 'We have found over the past two to three years that if we change an item – especially food – to our own label we always do better with it.'

The brand illuminates international sales. The company now has branded areas in many of the main food halls of Europe and is working on potential deals with the Far East and Middle East. Sales in the USA are also growing.

Fortnum & Mason's other big growth area – also boosting worldwide sales – is through the Internet. Again, the brand is crucial. As Beverley Aspinall says: 'Our brand was principally marketed in the UK, but increasingly with the global portal it is growing very strongly. It's quite complicated with food regulations, sell-by dates, warehousing, shipping, etc., but you can't let that defeat you.'

Again, the brand comes into its own for special events. In 2012 the Queen marks her Diamond Jubilee; as royal warrant holders, so will Fortnum's.

(Excerpt from *Professional Manager* magazine, May 2010.)

Protecting the brand in tough times

Understanding the sources of sustainable competitive advantage is even more important in a recession. Managers need to ensure these areas are not just protected from cuts but also invested in so that the brand remains strong. This can be difficult for managers to justify at a time when they are being asked to deliver more with less. But the key is to remember that for every challenge, there is also an opportunity.

A reduced budget doesn't have to result in a diluted brand. Often, it can actually be the stimulus for finding new and different ways of doing things. Going back to brand values is a good way to get guidance when it comes to making difficult decisions about where to cut and where to invest. If a key brand value is about leading-edge thinking, for example, managers need to retain their investment in developing people. If outstanding customer service is a central part of the business offering, managers must protect those activities that affect the company's ability to respond and deliver.

When times are turbulent, it's also vital to ensure that the organisation is managing internal and external messages simultaneously. Internal chaos will soon spill over to the outside world and can cause irreparable damage to the brand. Take the example of BA in summer 2010, when even the slightest whiff of industrial action caused people to switch airlines without delay. Once lost, customers can be very difficult to win back.

In a climate where there is the threat of redundancies or people are being asked to take pay cuts or reduce their hours, managers need to bring communication to the fore. In this scenario, the old-style team and cascade briefings no longer fit the bill. People need the opportunity to enter into a dialogue to discuss issues and get feedback.

Managers need to use all the communication channels at their disposal to keep people up to date and reinforce key messages about the kind of behaviour that will be valued. This will pay dividends in the long run. In tough times managers in businesses are far more likely to come up with new approaches and solutions to problems if they engage with employees than if they retreat to their offices.

PricewaterhouseCooper's approach to the need to cut its salary bill during the downturn is an excellent example of an organisation communicating well and protecting its brand, while also cutting its budget. The organisation's staff were all offered a range of options, from sabbaticals to part-time working, that would keep them in a job even though demand for services was low. Employees responded enthusiastically to the opportunity to avoid redundancy and the organisation was able to retain the skills of valuable employees so that it could maintain a high-quality service to clients and would be poised to seize opportunities for growth when the situation improved.

Checklist: Protecting the brand in tough times

- Take brand values into account when making difficult decisions about budget cuts.
- Involve employees in discussions about proposed reorganisation – those on the front line can help you assess the full impact and consequences of any changes.
- Create a two-way dialogue with your team. Actively seek their input on new ways of doing things.
- Ensure the business is conveying consistent messages to the inside and outside world.
- Take every opportunity to reinforce the brand values with your team so they are clear about the kind of behaviour that is desired.

Managing the brand online

The Internet has undoubtedly provided organisations with a powerful tool to promote their brand – but as many have learnt to their cost, it is a double-edged sword.

The growth of social networking and micro-blogging sites (Facebook, LinkedIn, Twitter et. al.) now means that anyone from a disgruntled consumer to an aggressive competitor can say exactly what they like about you online.

As David Woodward, writing in the June 2010 issue of *Director* magazine, says: 'Any customer with a complaint and a keyboard can now deliver their indelible verdict to a cast of billions.' Negative (and often inaccurate) stories can spread across the globe like wildfire. There are no controls, little opportunity for redress and damaging content is notoriously difficult to remove once published. A few clicks of the mouse and long-established corporate reputations can be irreparably damaged.

Managers' reluctance to fully embrace social media is, therefore, perfectly understandable. Indeed, there is often a tendency for those at the helm to try and actively prevent their employees from using this form of communication. The hard truth, however, is that the Internet and the social media it supports are here to stay – and organisations are better off engaging with them proactively rather than retreating behind a wall of silence.

The rules of engagement are, however, very different and managers need to make a significant shift in mindset before they can use social media to its full potential.

Letting go

Loss of control is often managers' biggest fear when it comes to social media. They are concerned that their employees may communicate with the outside world in ways that are 'off message' with the brand. They are worried that if they try and engage customers in a dialogue it will create unrealistic expectations or lead to unwarranted criticism of their products or services.

The reality, however, is that the traditional ways of communicating the brand are fast disappearing. It's no longer about pushing out carefully crafted corporate messages that only tell the outside world exactly what the organisation wants them to hear. Today's consumers expect a more interactive, dynamic and honest relationship with the brands they embrace.

Organisations need to recognise that managers often find it hard to step out of the controlled environments they have been used to and into this brave new world. They need to equip managers with the skills and confidence to manage social media successfully and to exploit the potential it offers to develop brands. The most successful organisations will be the ones that make social media an integral part of their communication strategy rather than as an afterthought or something that only happens in isolated pockets of the business where there are a few enthusiasts.

Developing a dialogue

One of the biggest differences between social media and traditional forms of communication is that they are two-way. This gives organisations an unprecedented opportunity to get customers fully engaged with the brand as opposed to seeing them as passive recipients of information.

Managers need to recognise that this is a gift. Yes, they will almost certainly not like everything they hear – but all feedback, negative or positive, is extremely valuable. It gives organisations a real-time snapshot of what their customers are thinking and feeling, and the chance to mould and tweak their offering accordingly.

The June 2010 issue of *Director* magazine reports on how pizza company Domino's used an open dialogue with its customers in response to a growing body of criticism about its products. The company shared feedback from a consumer focus group on YouTube, gave customers access to footage of its chefs as they made changes to the product and invited people to taste the new recipes. The business even set up an unmoderated comments section on its website where customers could freely leave feedback.

This is an excellent example of how social media can be used to generate engagement with a brand and build a 'community' of supportive and involved consumers. It was undoubtedly a brave strategy, but one that many other organisations could learn from.

Seizing opportunities

There is a tendency to regard social media as a threat, but managers need to recognise that they can also provide opportunities to build and develop their brand. Feedback from customers, for example, may act as the catalyst for developing new products or services. One of the key advantages of the opportunity for dialogue presented by social media is that they allow organisations to start a 'buzz' of excitement about new products before they are even ready for launch.

According to *Director* magazine, this is a strategy that has been successfully used by companies such as Vitaminwater, which invited its customers, via Facebook, to help it create a new flavour. Starbucks also built a customer portal, called myStarbucksidea, where customers were encouraged to give feedback on how its offering could be further developed.

Online forums and professional communities can also be the starting point for productive collaboration with other businesses in the same or complementary fields. Active participation in specialist forums can also help to establish the brand as a centre of expertise. This willingness to reach out and engage with others may come easily to younger managers who have grown up in the Internet age, but organisations need to recognise that others may need some support for their journey into unknown territory.

Responding to threats

It's a fact of life that most organisations will at some time come across unpalatable or inaccurate information that has been posted about them online. In more extreme circumstances, they may have to deal with a concerted campaign being waged against them by action or pressure groups. Both Nike and Nestlé, for example, have had to deal with long-running campaigns from protestors questioning their ethics, while supermarket groups frequently have to deal with local protest campaigns when they apply for planning permission to site new stores.

This is an area where managers need to think carefully about their strategy for protecting their reputation and communicating with the people they need to reach and influence. In his book *New Strategies for Reputation Management* (CIPR, 2008), Andrew Griffin suggests that companies need to take steps to regain the reputation initiative. This sometimes calls for courageous steps and standing up for what they believe is right – rather than being reactive and keeping a low profile.

Griffin argues that there is a need to change the corporate mindset from passive and apologetic to confident, assertive and (where required) combative. The key is to establish a strong and confident public position, rather than hiding from the issue and leaving the agenda (and the company's reputation) in the hands of others.

Traditionally, this protection of the company's reputation has remained firmly in the province of the communications department. Although they will naturally continue to take a lead, it is important for managers throughout the business to recognise that reputation lies at the heart of the organisation and that everyone in the business has a role to play in standing up for the brand in times of trouble.

Leader insight

The web can destroy corporate reputations with the pressing of a button.
John Taylor, Chief Executive, ACAS

Creating internal brand engagement

Of course brands do not exist in a vacuum. Leading brand consultancy Interbrand puts it succinctly: brands, it suggests, need to 'live in the hearts and minds of those who work for and with them. A company's workforce is the living embodiment of its brand in action. If they are engaged and energised they bring the brand to life.'

If a brand doesn't mean anything to the brand's employees, they will have trouble conveying messages and the meaning of the brand to the customer. This is especially true of service brands, the value of which often become tangible through human interaction – think about Singapore Airlines, FedEx and Starbucks, for example.

Many organisations approach this by establishing guidelines for 'on brand' behaviour. They provide information about how they would like employees to behave so that customers always experience the brand consistently and leave with a favourable impression.

Interbrand suggests, however, that there are some problems with this approach. First of all, it is difficult to come up with behavioural 'norms' that characterise a brand, over and above the usual standards of good customer service. Secondly, employees will not necessarily welcome attempts to make them 'conform' and suppress their individuality. 'The question boils down to this: if a brand is supposed to give customers something to identify with and add meaning to their lives, shouldn't helping employees express themselves as individuals help the brand as well?' says Interbrand Consulting Director Alexander Rauch.

He argues that if managed appropriately, employees intuitively become 'brand ambassadors' without ever having to learn a set of guidelines. The answer, once again, lies in values – and in helping employees see how their own values link in to those of the brand.

Managers need to facilitate this by making sure that there is an ongoing dialogue about what the brand stands for and how employees can apply these values to their work on a day-to-day basis. It's not a short-term initiative, but a long-term, continuous task of using the brand values to inspire and motivate people.

This calls for a level of communication that is alien to many organisations. They are still locked in the mindset that knowledge is power and are frightened to share too much information or seek feedback.

If employees are to truly buy into the brand, however, they need to be actively involved in its development. They need to feel free to 'think the unthinkable' and to raise questions about the way day-to-day transactions are handled and managed. This will lead to true engagement – and in many cases can also lead to powerful insights that transform the way the organisation goes about its business.

Checklist: Developing internal engagement

- Make sure you are exemplifying the brand values in the way you personally act and go about your day-to-day work.
- Open up the lines of communication with employees and actively encourage their involvement in developing the brand.
- Make sure you incorporate a brand perspective in performance reviews by giving employees feedback about how well they embody brand values in their work.
- Consider brand-driven incentive and bonus systems.
- Make sure brand values are reflected in recruitment and induction processes.
- Emphasise brand values during management development programmes and activities.

Case study: Cobra

(In his book *Against the Grain*, Cobra Beer founder Lord Karan Bilimoria describes how the business creates what he describes as 'The Cobra Buzz' ...)

> *'A good way of finding out just what kind of organisational culture a business has is to pay a visit to its headquarters. It doesn't matter what the values that are hanging on the wall say. They can proclaim that a company is a fun place to work in huge capital letters, but if the employees are wandering around with a miserable look fixed on their faces, it probably isn't.*
>
> *'Pay a visit to Cobra's headquarters, just around the corner from Parsons Green in London, and you should know immediately what kind of company you are dealing with. For a start, people look happy – busy but happy. The offices are open plan and there is continual interaction between the people working there. What*

*about the plush boss's office on the 15th floor? Not a chance. My
office is a few feet away from the rest of my employees, and the
door is usually open.*

*'Right there and then you get a sense of what Cobra is about
as an organisation: fun tempered with professionalism. Work has
got to be fun. There is absolutely no point otherwise. You have
got to enjoy what you are doing and you have got to like the
people you are with. You create an atmosphere where everyone
just gets on, and gets on well, and both they and you can feel it.'*

(From *Against the Grain: Lessons in Entrepreneurship from
the Founder of Cobra Beer*, Capstone, 2009.)

Engaging stakeholders in the brand

Managers also have a critical role to play in making sure all stakeholders
– such as customers, partners and suppliers – are fully engaged with the
brand. As we have seen earlier in this chapter, many organisations already
engage with their customers and use their feedback to help develop the
brand proposition. New and emerging channels of communication, such
as Twitter and Facebook, now provide an unprecedented opportunity for
organisations to enter into conversation with their customers.

There does, however, need to be clear and consistent communication with other stakeholders too. Yes, of course, there need to be sound
management processes in place to make sure that suppliers adhere to
their contracts and don't let the business (and therefore its customers)
down. But it's also important to have a regular, open and honest dialogue with suppliers so that any potential problems can be spotted and
dealt with early on. Would Gate Gourmet, for example, have been able
to cause such significant disruption to British Airways' operations during the long-running dispute over catering staff's pay and conditions if
the lines of communication had been fully open?

Partner organisations can also become influential ambassadors for the brand if managed in the right way. Managers need to make partners feel an important part of the brand 'family'. This means setting up mechanisms for regular dialogue, welcoming their feedback and ideas, and joining together to celebrate success.

Managers need to think carefully about the stakeholders who have the most important role to play in helping them build and protect their brand and reputation. The most important groups (those whose active support you need to operate) are often pushed down the priority list in favour of whose who appear on the surface to be more influential. (We talk in more detail about managing stakeholders in Chapter 4.)

It is also important to avoid brand dilution or brand damage through working with or through less scrupulous partners or suppliers. Particularly when times are tough, there can be a temptation to cut corners and to award contracts on cost alone. Such actions can permanently damage your brand.

Case study: Association of Chartered Certified Accountants (ACCA)

The ACCA is an excellent example of an organisation that has built a strong international brand with the help of its delivery partners. It is the leading provider of accountancy qualifications from entry through to professional level. Its qualifications are delivered around the world through a network of hundreds of delivery partners.

The association has been extremely successful in expanding its operations internationally due to the strong relationships it builds with qualification providers.

In many markets ACCA has established national offices that act as a key point of contact for relationships. Individual providers are also given access to a wealth of resources available from ACCA online. This helps them ensure they have the most up-to-date information and supports them in the development of their own individual businesses.

Sharing of best practice between delivery partners is actively encouraged and great emphasis is placed on celebrating the success of individuals who achieve ACCA qualifications.

This has allowed ACCA to create an extremely strong international brand and has helped it increase membership from 72,852 in March 2000 to 140,225 by March 2010.

Measuring brand equity

Putting a true value on a brand can be difficult – it is an intangible asset that is difficult to measure. Organisations do, however, need to put processes in place to evaluate their brand equity.

Leading branding consultancy Interbrand points out that branding is about differentiation, which can be tangible (e.g. product performance) or more emotional and symbolic (e.g. what it represents, what feelings it elicits). The sum of all the customers' associations, perceptions and feelings about a product's attributes, performance, brand name, symbols and the company associated with it gives equity to the brand.

Brand equity plays an important role in customers' purchase intentions and behaviour. Companies that track sources of brand equity, how they affect customer behaviour and how they change over time, are often steps ahead of the competition.

Qualitative and quantitative research techniques are used to identify sources of brand equity. Qualitative measures can help identify associations to a brand, its strength, favourability and uniqueness. Quantitative measures supplement this by providing a more solid ground for strategic and tactical recommendations. They act as a stethoscope to help organisations listen to the brand's heart and check how healthy it is.

Interbrand has now developed the world's first ISO certified approach for valuing brands. ISO 10668 sets minimum standard requirements for the procedures and methods used to determine the monetary value of brands. It sets out a coherent and reliable approach for brand valuation that takes into consideration financial, legal and behavioural science aspects.

Case study: Brand valuation at the Royal College of Art

The Royal College of Art (RCA) is the world's only postgraduate university of art and design. It has more than 900 masters and doctoral students, and more than 100 professionals and practitioners active in the college.

Interbrand's brand valuation formed part of a submission to the Higher Education Funding Council for England (HEFCE) to support the case for maintaining the college's existing funding levels and status. The RCA was also in the middle of a fundraising project, to finance a new campus for its Fine and Applied Arts departments.

The challenge was to devise a robust and defendable way to calculate the financial value of the brand, despite the not-for-profit nature of the college.

Because standard approaches for valuing brands require a profit forecast as a key input, Interbrand applied an adapted form of its methodology to assess the impact of the brand on future cash flows (rather than profits). They then calculated the financial value of the brand from this assessment.

The study showed that the RCA owns and manages powerful assets, which create an economic advantage. These assets include talented lecturers, a prestigious location in South Kensington, spacious buildings and of course a strong brand and reputation. Interbrand estimates that almost half of the college's economic advantage was attributable specifically to the brand.

The brand creates value by positively influencing the perceptions and behaviours of a variety of stakeholders, including students, staff, donors, businesses and specialist suppliers. It enables the RCA, through its impact on stakeholder behaviour, to command premium fees and enjoy lower costs of doing business.

Professor Jeremy Myerson, Director of Innovation at the RCA, said of the valuation: 'Until now, we have had no way of putting a monetary value on the very many intangible benefits that accrue to the college due to its international reputation. This valuation has been a robust financial exercise that shows how the RCA's brand gives the college an economic leverage.'

Key questions

- Do you need to develop your understanding of basic marketing and branding principles?
- Is your organisation exploiting its brand to the fullest possible extent?
- What specific opportunities are there for the business to reinforce and build on the strengths of its brand?
- Are your employees clear about the brand values and demonstrating them in their day-to-day dealings with customers?
- What efforts have you made to fully engage stakeholders in the brand?
- Are your partners acting as ambassadors for the brand? If not, what can you do to encourage them?
- Is feedback from customers actively sought and fully exploited?
- Do you have systems in place to measure brand equity?

In this chapter we have looked at the vital role that managers have to play in supporting their organisation's brand and protecting corporate reputation. As you have read, developing high levels of brand engagement internally has been key to the success of many top brands. Many organisations have chosen to make embracing diversity an important part of their brand offering. In Chapter 9 we go on to look at the important role that managers have to play in exploiting the diverse talents in their workforce.

CHAPTER 9

Good diversity practices should not be seen as an overhead, but I suspect they sometimes are – particularly when times are tough.
Phillippa Williamson, Chief Executive, Serious Fraud Office

Effective management of diversity is one of the biggest challenges facing organisations today, and probably the issue that also causes the most difficulty and discomfort for managers on the front line.

There's no question that organisations that successfully exploit the diverse talents in their workforce are always going to be ahead of the game. They will be better placed to compete on the global stage, better equipped to understand and capture new markets, and more able to maximise opportunities as we emerge from recession. Sadly, however, many organisations have not yet recognised the power they can leverage from a positive approach to managing diversity.

The Chartered Management Institute's (CMI's) position on this is that while we are not in favour of discrimination, we are in favour of positive actions. Why?

The problem is twofold:

- In many businesses, working practices have not evolved in tandem with the changes taking place in our society. Women now make up 46% of the UK's workforce, ethnic minorities account for an estimated 90% of the growth in the working age population and more than a quarter of people in the workforce are aged 50 or over. Yet organisations still persist in rigid, inflexible ways of working that are completely out of tune with the desires, needs and lifestyles of these valuable employees.
- Diversity has become hopelessly mixed up with the human rights and political agenda. Yes, of course, we all want an equal society where human rights are respected and people are treated fairly. But we also need a responsive, fast-moving economy where the skills, talents and potential of all employees are maximised to the full. In many cases, managers have become so frightened of putting a foot wrong and falling foul of the legislation that they have become blinkered to the fact there is a pressing business case for managing diversity effectively.

Leaders and managers need to stop thinking about diversity in terms of compliance with the regulations and start thinking about how they can attract, motivate and retain the diverse talent that will help them achieve sustainable business growth. This shift in mindset is even more important in difficult economic times, when having the right skills and knowledge can give an organisation a much-needed competitive edge.

Positive management of diversity can help to:

- Realise and develop potential that already exists within the workforce
- Improve the motivation and commitment of employees

- Improve morale and job satisfaction, leading to greater productivity
- Reduce labour turnover, leading to reduced recruitment and training costs
- Increase the flow of ideas, leading to greater creativity and innovation
- Create greater flexibility within the workforce
- Ensure that organisations comply with the requirements of equal opportunities legislation and eliminate discriminatory behaviour
- Produce a workforce that is better-equipped to serve a diverse customer base and diverse markets, leading to high levels of customer satisfaction
- Improve an organisation's ability to compete in global markets
- Enhance the organisation's corporate image as it is seen as a socially responsible employer.

If we are to prosper in the 21st century we must create a working culture that harnesses the talents of the widest possible range of people. Britain cannot afford to go on asking employees to fit their families around the demands of ever-more intense 24/7 global competition, and marginalising or rejecting workers who fail to fit into traditional and inflexible working arrangements.

Two Years Making Changes, Equality and
Human Rights Commission report

Leader insights

Too often I worry that we regard ourselves as 'accommodating' diversity when we must learn to celebrate it and use diverse perspectives and talents as an opportunity.

Steve Holliday, Chief Executive, National Grid

> *There are still a lot of hidden barriers. The business case has been overused so that when business is down, companies feel able to ignore diversity issues. This is a problem.*
>
> Nigel Meager, Director, Institute for Employment Studies (IES)
>
> *The challenge is cultural, not legislative, and setting targets won't necessarily change practices.*
>
> Stefan Stern, Director of Strategy, Edelman

Diversity – the true picture

Mention the word 'diversity' and most people will instantly think of race or religion. The true picture is of course much wider. The EHRC recognises seven strands of diversity: age, disability, gender, race, religion and belief, sexual orientation and gender reassignment.

Organisations that seek to proactively manage diversity need to embrace all these groups – but from a business standpoint, the definition needs to be even wider. A truly diverse workforce will:

- Encompass different cultures
- Include a blend of youth and experience
- Embrace people of different social backgrounds and personality types.

In an ideal scenario, this mix should exist at every rank and level, from the most senior managers through to new recruits entering the world of work for the first time.

Statistics show that this situation is far from reality in many organisations. Representation of women at senior level is still appalling, with the proportion of women on FTSE 100 boards standing at just 12.5%.

Research has shown that at the current rate, it will take another 27 years to achieve equality in civil service top management, another 55 years to achieve an equal number of senior women in the judiciary and around 200 years to achieve an equal number of women in Parliament. On average it will take another 57 years to achieve equal pay for men and women at the current rate of progress. Very few government ministers or indeed employers would accept this as a desirable state of affairs.

Research conducted by the CMI shows that under-representation is a serious issue among other minority groups too. Its report *Management Recruitment: Understanding Greater Routes to Diversity* shows that although there are high levels of ambition among under-represented groups, these aspirations are not being effectively supported in the workplace.

Survey respondents – who included women, people with long-term health conditions or disability and those from ethnic minority groups – were asked to identify the barriers they felt were holding them back. Almost a quarter mentioned the existence of the 'old boy' network; two in ten highlighted family commitments; and one in ten cited racial discrimination. Barriers to progression appeared to be even more entrenched at the top end of the scale. When it came to board-level appointments, the majority agreed you have to 'know the right person' (65%) and that cultural fit was important (64%). Only 38% of managers agreed that candidates from diverse backgrounds were encouraged and less than a quarter felt the selection process for senior appointments was open and transparent.

UK plc scores badly when it comes to age diversity too. Joint research by the CMI and the Chartered Institute of Personnel and Development (CIPD) showed that despite the decline in the number of young people set to enter the workforce, many organisations have no strategy in place for managing an ageing workforce. Only 14% of those surveyed considered their organisation was well-prepared for the issues likely to be presented by a 'greying' employee base. Only 7% of organisations offered training to line managers on managing older workers, although 47% felt training was needed and 59% thought young managers found it hard to manage older workers (*Managing an Ageing Workforce: How Employers are Adapting to an Older Labour Market*, CMI and CIPD, 2010).

There is also an enormous lack of understanding about disability, which – despite strenuous efforts by charities and pressure groups working in the field – is still perceived by many as meaning 'a person in a wheelchair'. Only one in four disabled people are in employment, which is a huge waste of skills and talent and a vastly under-utilised resource.

Leader insights

Only one in ten people with a learning disability work. We need to take this issue seriously.

Jill Tombs, Director of Human Resources and Governance,

Mencap

You never know where you are going to find the right person. It doesn't necessarily have to be through a recruitment agency and it doesn't have to be through an advert in the Evening Standard. We have recruited some of our best people through a wide variety of sources.

Lord Bilimoria, Chairman, Cobra Beer Partnership

Managers need to emerge from their silos and start to widen their understanding of what diversity really means and just how much untapped potential they have at their disposal. Even at a time when redundancies are rife, businesses are still facing severe skills shortages, particularly in technical skills, engineering and medicine, but also in the more generic management and leadership skills.

Life itself is diverse and dynamic. A key task for leaders and managers is to find new and creative ways of overcoming the barriers to diversity so that their workforces can begin to reflect the reality of the rich, varied and multicultural world we now live in.

Leader insights

There are too many excluded groups in the UK, despite hard work over the years to reduce inequality. There are important social changes taking place and we need to encourage all our managers and leaders in the three sectors of our economy to be tolerant and appreciative of each other. We need everyone to be part of the talent pool.

Martin Bean, Vice Chancellor, The Open University

We need to motivate those who are alienated from our society and who are on the periphery.

Lord Bichard, founder, Institute for Government

The most creative organisations are those with diversity – people from different backgrounds, genders, ethnicity and education. We should encourage diversity not just to make us more inclusive but to make us more creative.

Andrew Summers, Chairman of the Steering Board, Companies House

Case study: Managing age diversity at Dyfed-Powys Police

Our aim is to reflect through our staff internally the communities we serve externally, across all the diversity strands.

Chief Superintendent Gwyn Thomas, Dyfed-Powys Police

In its quest to reflect the communities it serves, Dyfed-Powys Police has established working groups for each of the diversity strands identified in its Single Equality Scheme. These groups are each led by senior managers who act as champions, promoting the needs of the different diversity strands – including one dedicated to promoting pro-age agendas. Group leads are influential senior police officers and staff able to influence the organisation at strategic level.

Thomas believes that encouraging older and younger employees to work together can promote better understanding between each group's needs and perspective. Diverse teams with members of varying ages enable them to better engage with and serve the differing needs of the many rural communities that are served by Dyfed-Powys Police Service.

Police pension regulations currently mean that police officers of the rank of Constable and Sergeant have to retire by the age of 55; however, police staff work to the statutory retirement age of 65. (This is currently under review in line with UK government direction.) Older workers, especially those over 50, are considered both committed and stable employees. There are examples of Police Community Support Officers (PCSOs), in particular, being recruited in their 50s, and some of these are retired police officers rejoining the force.

Dyfed-Powys Police takes great pride in its occupational health services, which proactively offer services to support and monitor the health and fitness of officers and staff. Proactive policies, such as leadership training that focuses on employee wellbeing and the promotion of healthy lifestyles, are seen as integral to the success of the organisation. A variety of flexible and part-time working arrangements are offered to employees and this is seen as a key factor in enabling the service to get the best out of all its employees in serving the rural communities of Dyfed & Powys.

(From *Managing an Ageing Workforce: How Employers are Adapting to an Older Labour Market*, CMI/CIPD, September 2010.)

Checklist: Key questions to ask yourself about diversity

- Is the selection process for senior appointments open and transparent?
- Are you providing training and support for line managers in how to effectively manage older workers?
- Is the prevailing culture in your team welcoming of people from different cultures and backgrounds?
- Have you investigated the full range of flexible working options on offer and assessed how these could be implemented in your team?
- How can you widen the net when it comes to recruitment and look for suitable candidates outside of the normal channels?
- Have you considered recruiting for attitude and training for skills to avoid building a team of corporate clones?
- Are the role models you are promoting internally inspiring or exhausting?
- Do special interests groups in the business link their activities into corporate goals and objectives?

Overcoming the barriers to diversity

The barriers to diversity will vary from business to business. Some, such as prejudicial attitudes, are overt, while others lie under the surface. These hidden barriers, which exist in most organisations to some degree, are often the ones that impede progress the most. Managers and leaders need to put their policies and practices under the microscope to make sure they are not unwittingly hampering efforts to encourage diversity.

Inappropriate recruitment practices

Managers have a tendency to see the job in terms of the current role holder. The problem with this approach is that there is a danger of creating corporate 'clones' who will look at issues and challenges in exactly the same way as their predecessors, therefore producing exactly the same result. Instead of moving forward, the organisation stands still. As the old adage goes: 'If you always do what you always did, you'll always get what you always got'.

Managers need to widen their perspective when it comes to recruitment and get out of the mindset of hiring people who 'fit in' and are 'just like me'. One way to achieve this is to recruit for attitude and train for skills. A candidate may, for example, come from a very different background and not have the exact skills you require, but maybe they have shown that they have managed a significant change project or developed a whole new service, albeit in a different setting. Someone who can shed a new light on an old situation, and who has demonstrated an ability to successfully develop competency in the past, is likely to be a much more powerful candidate than someone who has done the same job, in the same way, for many years.

A good illustration of this is the decision some time ago by the National Society for Prevention of Cruelty to Children (NSPCC) to recruit fundraisers internally from its pool of front-line workers rather than bringing people with specialist skills in from outside. It found that those who understood the reality of working with disadvantaged children and families could convey that story much more effectively to potential donors, and were more effective at getting the funds rolling in. All they needed was a little bit of additional development on the technicalities and techniques of the fundraising process.

If managers are to attract a diverse pool of candidates, they may also need to rethink some of the more traditional ways of advertising jobs and find creative ways of communicating with the people they want to attract.

The following example, from Tower Hamlets, is a good example of how to build a workforce that mirrors the diverse community it serves.

Case study: Building a workforce that is fully reflective of the community at NHS Tower Hamlets

What our organisation is about
NHS Tower Hamlet's key aim is to improve the health and well-being of local people living in Tower Hamlets in East London. We want to reduce inequalities in health and improve services for local people.

We are focused on all six strands of equality – race, authenticity, gender, disability, religion, sexual orientation and age – and they all interrelate with each other. We have a set of targets and priorities for each of these areas. There is a very lively discussion currently going on in the organisation about how each of these strands relate to one another. A key issue is having a workforce that is fully reflective of the community that we serve. What is talent management and diversity about from Tower Hamlets' perspective?

'I view talent and diversity as completely linked.'

It is not correct to say that they are at odds with each other because having a diverse workforce is the same as having a talented workforce and having a talented workforce must be diverse, so the two go together hand in hand. What I say to people in Tower Hamlets is that we want to recruit the very, very best talent that is available and we want to recruit the widest range of different kinds of people and local people and those two things aren't mutually exclusive. They are the same thing.

The targets and measures we use
Some of the measures/targets we use are part of the local government regime that is called 'best value' – all local authorities have got targets around gender, race and disability, and so with those we aim to get

ourselves into the upper quartile in comparison with other local authorities. If that is not really a relevant comparison, then we look at what's in the community that we are serving and we match ourselves to that.

The council's cabinet has a report on progress every six months. It's very high profile and the elected members of the council are very committed to achieving progress against the targets. They are younger than average, very diverse, more likely to be in full-time employment and very community-focused. They understand what the issues are about. The NHS board is similarly committed and interested, and looking for evidence of progress.

We track how many of our employees live locally, we capture their postcode, we capture promotions, we capture the profile of our workforce against the six equality strands, and we track the people who applied, how many from each area were shortlisted and how many were appointed.

Talent and diversity initiatives/programmes

Career café: We recently held a big event for about 150 of our diverse leaders' network who have been through our talent programmes. We called it a 'career cafe' and the purpose was to get them to take a bit more responsibility for managing their own careers. We had speakers who gave examples of what they have done in their lives and also from some high-powered headhunters who described what they are looking for, how you need to evidence your experience and the tools to move up the organisation.

Keep diverse talent warm: We are currently partnering with another organisation to identify people that we would want to recruit into Tower Hamlets, even if we haven't got a job for them at the moment. We make contact, give them a tour of the borough, introduce them to some of the leading figures and keep them warmed and informed about what's going on in Tower Hamlets. This means that when a job comes up they think 'I know that they are diversity-friendly, I understand what they are about, I can apply for this job'.

Talent programmes: We have a host of different talent and diversity schemes, such as the Hamlets Youth Scheme and different graduate programmes linked to professional career paths. We also have positive action programmes for aspiring leaders and middle managers. We have also recently held a 'career cafe' for 150 of our diverse leaders' network, aimed at getting them to take more responsibility for managing their own careers and to think about what is needed to move up the organisation.

Developing internal talent: We try to fill most senior posts from the talent that we have already got internally because we are a very diverse workforce. We've trained people up, we have identified the stars, we give them opportunities to act up, so if you are a betting person you are probably going to say that it is going to be an internal promotion. However, we still have to try to identify what talent out there would help us to achieve our targets while not compromising on having the very best that's available. We advertise nationally for roles, but we also always advertise locally.

Although we are focused on getting local people into employment we are also focused on getting the very best that we can – we try and do the two together.

My advice

1 Philosophically reconcile yourself to the fact that talent and diversity must be interlinked.

2 Be really clear about what you want to achieve and have a really practical plan to get you there.

3 Get the buy-in and commitment of your leadership team.

4 Recognise that talent and diversity are business imperatives and have to be driven by the business.

5 Monitor your progress – know where you are and where you want to get to.

(By Deborah Clarke, Director of Human Resources and Organisation Development; from *Opening up Talent for Business Success: Integrating Talent Management and Diversity*, CIPD.)

Leader insights

It is not a good idea to create organisational norms or clones, and people need permission to be themselves if they are to be most effective.

Helen Brand, CEO, Association of Chartered Certified Accountants (ACCA)

It is all too easy for employers to filter out candidates on the basis of the face not fitting.

Mark Turner, Senior Partner, GatenbySanderson

Too many people make decisions based on stereotypes without knowing it.

Penny De Valk, Chief Executive Officer, Institute of Leadership and Management

Presenteeism

We have highlighted the problem of inflexible working practices earlier, but a culture of presenteeism can have an equally negative effect on efforts to encourage diversity. The 'jacket over the chair' syndrome of the 1980s sadly still exists in some organisations, with employees expected to work ever longer hours, particularly in difficult times like these when jobs are being cut and a diminishing number of people have to cope with the same amount of work. Ironically, the availability of technology has worsened rather than eased this problem. It seems there is no now escape, with harassed employees often expected to be at the beck and call of managers or clients 24/7 via their BlackBerry or iPhone.

This kind of culture is not conducive to effective working; people don't perform at their peak when they are tired and stressed. It is also likely to work against employees (both male and female) with family and caring responsibilities who need to know that they can go home on time at the end of the working day.

Managers and leaders need to take a step back and make sure that they are rewarding people for contribution made rather than hours spent. They need to ensure leaving on time is not frowned at in their teams and to insist that lunch is not a luxury!

Lack of role models

Much has been written elsewhere about the lack of role models at the top. There is no doubt that organisations need both more women and more representatives from ethnic minority groups at the helm of organisations. Good diversity practice needs to be led from the top and organisations cannot claim to be committed to diversity if this is not reflected in their senior management team.

Recent research from the US shows the importance of role models who can also act as sponsors to talented individuals and thus change those diversity statistics at the top (*Synergies at the Cutting Edge: The Sponsor Effect*, 2010, Center for Work-Life Policy).

There is an interesting dichotomy, however, in the way organisations tend to portray the role models they do have in an attempt to show others that getting to the top is achievable. This is particularly true of the way business tends to present senior women. How often have you read articles demonstrating how a high-flying female executive gets up at 5 a.m., checks her BlackBerry and answers some emails, makes the packed lunch and gets the children off to school, dives into her first meeting at 8 a.m. (looking immaculately groomed, of course), and manages to get home in time to run her children's bath and read them a bedtime story?

This catalogue of activities is exhausting to read and quite frankly not particularly inspirational for the majority of already hard-pressed working women. 'Why on earth would I want to do that?' is more likely to be the reaction from a female manager who is considering her next move up the corporate ladder. We have created a monster called 'Superwoman' and we are now paying for it – witnessed by the droves of women who are leaving full-time employment in the corporate world to set up their own, far more flexible family-friendly businesses.

If organisations are to retain and maximise the potential of valuable female employees, they need to look at the way work is organised and, on occasions, adapt roles to make them more appealing and achievable for women.

Tim Melville-Ross, Group Chairman of DTZ Holdings plc, describes how Nationwide, following its merger with the Anglia, made it easier for female managers to gain promotion. The business realised that the practice of moving managers from one branch to a (usually larger) branch on their way up the management ladder was acting as a barrier for many women with young families. Changes were made to this policy and, as a result, there was a significant increase in the number of female branch managers coming through.

Leader insight

We don't help women with families to manage at home and at work. As a result, we are not maximising the ROI.
    Tim Melville-Ross, Group Chairman, DTZ Holdings plc

Case study: Part-time working at Allen & Overy

(Geoff Fuller is a partner at law firm Allen & Overy. In early 2010 the organisation introduced formal arrangements for full equity partners to work part-time, in an effort to retain more women through to partnership. His thoughts on these developments are below.)

As one of the leading international law firms in the world, it's incredibly important for us to attract and retain the best talent. This means we need to encourage both men and women to progress right the way through to senior level. There is often a perception within the legal industry that partners' demanding workload is incompatible with having a family. This is a serious issue for us, as people often want to start a family just when they are ready to become a partner. We don't want to lose or put off our most talented people from considering partnership, so we've adapted our business model to offer part-time working.

Last year 62% of our UK graduate intake was female. If we don't succeed in attracting more women through to partner we will be choosing from an ever-decreasing pool of talent. Our arrangements mean partners can now choose to work a minimum of four days a week or be entitled to a maximum of 52 days' extra leave a year, allowing them to spend time with their children without having to sacrifice their careers. Employees at more junior levels can also benefit from term-time working, job-sharing, home working, increased paternity leave and emergency childcare, allowing staff to achieve a better balance between work and home life.

Although we appreciate flexible working is by no means a 'silver bullet' or cure-all approach, so far the response has been incredibly positive. We now have partners working part-time in nearly every practice group throughout the business and the scheme has been adopted in a number of different countries. Our clients, many of whom are women, have welcomed these steps and want to be seen to be associated with a law firm that respects the needs of its people.

Unhelpful divisions

There has been a tendency in the past for organisations to carve themselves up into 'groups'. It's not uncommon, particularly in large organisations, to see groups representing gay and lesbian workers, senior women, or Afro-Caribbean employees, for example. Although these special interest groups can be helpful in providing a forum where employees can share experiences and concerns, they can be divisive if they are not managed carefully. Diversity is about inclusiveness and organisations need to make sure they are not reinforcing differences or falling into a 'them and us' mindset.

A key task for leaders and managers is to make sure that minority groups are managed in a way that brings diverse communities together both for the benefit of employees and for the good of the business.

One approach that has been successfully used is to require groups to put together a business plan with key objectives that link into the overall corporate strategy. Groups are then given the opportunity to bid for funds to carry forward specific projects and activities. This approach can be successful in helping businesses strengthen relationships with key groups of employees, gain a deeper insight into the needs of different cultures and communities, and gain entry into new and emerging markets.

Taking diversity forward

A strategic approach to managing diversity will help organisations widen their talent base and get the best from the mix of experience and perspectives they have at their disposal.

The following checklist outlines the key stages of an effective diversity management programme.

 Checklist: Managing diversity

- **Set realistic goals:** Make sure you have specific and achievable goals for your diversity management programme. Objectives will vary depending on circumstances, but some examples might be to:
  - Increase the proportion of women in the workforce to 50%
  - Enable more flexible working practices, such as more home-working

- Facilitate recruitment from a wider geographical or cultural area.

  Whatever goals are set, it's important to relate them to the organisation's overall vision and mission statement, and to make sure they are linked to any other significant organisational initiatives. Make sure there is commitment to the goals from the top.

- **Gauge existing levels of diversity:** Find out what kind of differences affect the ability of individuals to achieve their potential in your organisation. To what extent do these differences create disadvantages or advantages for employees? How do organisational procedures and strategies affect different groups of employees? You can gather this information via a variety of means, which might include confidential questionnaires, individual interviews or focus group discussions. It can also be helpful to review all the documentary evidence you already have (e.g. policies, procedures, recruitment data) and to benchmark against organisations similar to your own. This will help you find examples of best practice to follow and of bad practice to avoid.

- **Identify areas where change is needed:** Once you have all the information to hand, you can start to look at areas where change is needed. Some of these may be small, incremental changes; others may require significant changes to policy. You might find you need to make changes to recruitment procedure, for example, or to introduce new and more flexible working arrangements. Action may be needed to combat prejudice or improve intercultural communication, or perhaps you might need to make changes to the physical environment so that there is better access for disabled workers and customers. Make sure you consult widely about any proposed changes rather than imposing them from on high.

- **Develop a diversity policy:** A written diversity policy can ensure everyone knows what diversity means in your business and what they personally need to do about it. A typical policy might include a definition of diversity, the reasons why it is important, the goals of the diversity management programme and information about the ways in which these goals will be achieved.

- **Identify facilitators:** Identify diversity 'champions', in other words facilitators who can act as change agents to lead initiatives and cascade them throughout your organisation or team.
- **Communicate and engage:** Make sure everyone in the business knows and understands what you are trying to achieve and has the opportunity to contribute their own ideas. If employees feel they have had an input, they are much more likely to give their whole-hearted backing and commitment to any initiatives you want to drive through or changes you want to make.
- **Provide training and support for managers:** Managers often need help to feel confident and competent to manage people from different cultures. People who are able to behave naturally, even if they get it wrong, get forgiven, especially if they have already developed good rapport. Multicultural awareness sessions, individual coaching and focus/discussion groups are all techniques that will help managers gain confidence, build rapport and reduce conflict within their teams.
- **Support managers from under-represented communities:** Make sure you are providing access to management and leadership opportunities to managers from all backgrounds. Ensure that the delivery and format is not unintentionally excluding those from under-represented groups. Mentoring and buddying is also an effective way of helping people gain confidence and develop higher level skills.

- **Help managers find internal role models/sponsors:** Consider setting up a network of 'sponsors' who can help managers from under-represented groups gain greater visibility, access career development opportunities and make the right connections with senior people.
- Enable the brightest people in your organisation to accelerate their own learning by giving them projects to run.

Leader insight

I'm a passionate advocate of fostering diversity in organisations; it is a huge competitive advantage. I know this from experience. ... As CEO I would sometimes refer to my management team as a mini United Nations, and within Cobra there is diversity across the spectrum, from age to expertise, from faith to country of origin. That diversity is reflected throughout the Cobra organisation. We have more than 20 different nationalities represented, people from Britain, Spain, Poland, India, Pakistan, Bangladesh, Sri Lanka, South Africa, Kenya, Canada ... people from all over the world. It is so enriching, because it creates a balance and this huge variety of backgrounds and approaches and mindsets all come together. It is a huge advantage for a business to have.

Lord Bilimoria, Chairman, Cobra Beer Partnership, in
*Against the Grain: Lessons in Entrepreneurship from
the Founder of Cobra Beer*, Capstone, 2009

Key questions

- Are we checking out our attractiveness to diverse recruits?
- Is the pay/benefits/training package targeted toward specific groups?
- Does it take too long to get from the bottom to the middle to the top?
- Are there diverse role models?
- Are we advertising all jobs at all levels as job share/part-time?
- Are we gathering quantitative evidence from exit interviews?
- What career planning are you offering our people?
- What kind of job rotation/flexibility is possible in the company?
- Are we offering mentoring/coaching into new job roles?
- Are we offering opportunities for continuous professional development and time away from the coalface for personalised learning?

In this chapter we have given practical guidance on the steps that managers need to take to fully embrace and take advantage of the diverse talent in their organisations. In the next and final chapter, we look at the challenges likely to face managers in the future and provide a round-up of the key points highlighted in each section.

CHAPTER 10

The need for managers to raise their game to an unprecedented level is the stark message that jumps out of the pages of this book.

Swathes of management jobs are being cut in both the public and the private sector. It is estimated that 46 000 posts will be lost in the NHS alone, many of them managerial roles. At the same time, the UK Commission for Education and Skills is telling us that 802 000 more managers will be needed by 2017.

Managers have become the jam that is being squeezed in the middle of this sandwich. They are being asked to take on a wider variety of tasks and to achieve more stretching targets with less and less support and resources. This has big implications for the way that managers approach their role and for the skills they will need going forward.

As we move towards greater deregulation, it will become increasingly important for future leaders to take a strong values-driven approach to their roles. One of the key leadership competences will be the ability to take a vision and make it immediate and accessible so that people are not left guessing about what they need to do – and, more importantly, how they need to do it.

The need for an unprecedented level of transparency has been brought about partly by the Internet, which has meant that there are no longer any secret corners for organisations to hide in. Managers need to be proud of what they do and the way they go about their business, and leaders need to make sure that this honest, open and ethical approach permeates every part of the organisation.

On a practical level, the pace of change and the need for more accountability has a big bearing on the specific skills that managers need to develop. As you will have seen in this book, tomorrow's manager will need to significantly expand their toolkit.

- Both public and private sector managers will need to acquire the skills to manage a wide range of stakeholders, attract and retain a diverse range of talent, and consider the impact of their activities on the environment.
- The ability to drive innovation has become increasingly important too, as consumers become more demanding and competition intensifies. Managers need to get more radical and transformative in their thinking about new products and the way they are delivered and priced. It is no longer enough to simply tinker with the product and cut a few corners to bring the cost down; tomorrow's managers will need to find new and completely different ways of meeting consumer demands.
- Partnership working is another area that is increasingly coming to the fore. As the 'Berlin Wall' between public and private sector comes tumbling down, we are already seeing more collaborative projects taking place. However, the skills and competences that go with partnership working are often poorly developed and will need significant attention – otherwise there is a risk there will be poor delivery, poor execution and a perception that low value is being added.
- Thanks to cuts in public sector budgets, there will be more outsourcing of contracts to the voluntary sector too. This means that the skills of procurement and contract management will become a more important part of the manager's armoury.

In addition to these core areas, there is an overall need for managers to improve the level of their soft skills. Expertise in communication and relationship-building will be necessary if managers are to lead teams of often disgruntled employees through yet more change. Negotiation and conflict management skills will also become a valuable asset – witness the rise we are already seeing in industrial action. The question that UK plc needs to ask itself is how well managers already in the system are equipped with these important skills. Experience suggests that there is a long way to go before management competence catches up with the challenges that managers are being asked to deal with.

We need to get serious about investment in management development; after all, organisations cannot expect their people to deliver if they have not equipped them for the task in hand. My view is that in the years ahead we are likely to see more outsourcing of management development activity as organisations look for cost-effective ways of keeping their people up to date. The pace of work is also likely to mean a continued trend away from traditional management education towards open, flexible, bite-sized learning that takes place throughout managers' careers.

Organisations will have to think carefully about the way they manage their talent, too. We are already facing serious skills shortages – and, with fewer young people due to enter the workforce, managers will have to make sure they exploit the skills of existing employees to the full.

This will mean that managers will have to widen their perspective about the type of people they need to fulfil specific roles, and in particular pay more attention to the way they utilise older workers and encourage women to play a more significant part in the workforce. My belief is that we need to make a shift towards hiring for attitude and training for skills, rather than focusing solely on experience-based recruitment. This will give organisations access to a pool of talent they probably never even realised they had.

In the difficult years ahead I believe we will also see a rise in the demand for interim managers who can fulfil short-term, specialist needs. Consultancy is also likely to experience an upturn, although the larger consultancy firms will have to work hard to find more innovative and cost-effective solutions for their clients.

Finally, I believe we need to do more to facilitate the transfer of talent between the public and private sectors in order to encourage some much-needed cross-fertilisation and sharing of experience. This will require a significant mindshift on the part of managers, who need to be encouraged to take a less blinkered attitude and look for competence that can be transferred.

What this book has demonstrated is that the management job just got a whole lot more complicated – however, the rewards for organisations that help their people surmount the challenges will be immense.

On values

Managers need to put values and ethics at the heart of everything they do. They need to walk the talk and help employees understand how they can link their own personal values to corporate objectives. Accountability and transparency need to rise to the very top of the agenda, and managers must find frameworks that will help them monitor their ethical performance.

On managing yourself and others

Managers need to devote sufficient time and attention to developing self-awareness and enhancing their personal toolkit of skills and competencies. Leaders must learn to adapt their leadership style to suit the circumstances. They need to shift the focus to meeting standards rather than achieving targets and be equally prepared to accept responsibility for failure as well as to celebrate success.

On managing change and uncertainty

Managers need to develop the skills to build cultures that are more accepting of change. They need a high level of influencing and communication skills to help deal with internal politics and gain commitment, support and engagement from their teams for the many and constant changes that lie ahead.

On managing stakeholders

The ability to manage stakeholders well has never been more important. Managers need to improve their understanding of stakeholders and how they interact with each other. High-level soft skills are required if managers are to effectively influence and engage with stakeholders and use their involvement to drive improved performance.

On risk and business continuity

Organisations urgently need to improve their preparedness for managing risk and ensuring business continuity. Managers need to shift away from the mindset where risk is about compliance and solving problems, towards an understanding that it is a key business tool that can help them improve performance.

On managing the environment

Organisations need to make 'green' behaviour an integral part of everything they do. Managers need to increase their understanding of how to proactively manage with the environment in mind. They need to work on developing management practices that will help us make better use of finite resources.

On managing innovation

Managers need to develop their understanding of how to stimulate innovative thinking and help their teams put new and creative ideas into practice. They need to break down the barriers that typically exist in organisations and find ways of opening the door to radical and transformative thinking.

On managing brand and reputation

This cannot be left to the marketing specialists alone. Managers need to develop their understanding of how they can help to fully exploit and develop their organisation's brand. They also need to hone high-level communication skills to help secure employee engagement with the brand, allowing them to embrace the new online world.

On managing diversity

Managers need to learn how to exploit and embrace the diverse talents in their workforce. They need to shift their focus from one of compliance with legislation towards a more in-depth understanding of how diversity can help them exploit new markets and achieve sustainable business growth.

CMI Management Checklists, Research and Best Practice Guides are available free of charge to CMI members and can be downloaded from our website at www.managers.org.uk. Non-members may purchase copies of our checklists and other resources via the 'Products & services' section of our website. You can find out about membership of the CMI at www.managers.org.uk/membership.

Chapter 1: Values and ethics

CMI management checklists

Codes of ethics (Checklist 028)
Corporate social responsibility (Checklist 242)
Producing a corporate mission statement (Checklist 067)

Other resources

Chartered Management Institute. *Code of Professional Conduct and Practice*. London: 2010
Lucas, Erika. 'Learning with a helping hand'. *Professional Manager*, September 2009, pp. 22–5

Macleod, Alison. *Generation Y: Unlocking the Talent of Young Managers.* London: Chartered Management Institute, 2008

Organisations

Chartered Institute of Personnel and Development (www.cipd.co.uk)
Investors in People (www.investorsinpeople.co.uk)
National Council for Voluntary Organisations (www.ncvo-vol.org.uk)

Chapter 2: Managing yourself and leading others

CMI management checklists

Developing trust (Checklist 243)
Emotional intelligence (Checklist 178)
Handling information – avoiding overload (Checklist 150)
Leading from the middle (Checklist 041)
Managing your time effectively (Checklist 016)
Personal development planning (Checklist 092)
Testing for personal effectiveness (Checklist 164)
Understanding management styles (Checklist 236)

Other resources

Bird, Polly. *Time Management* (Instant Manager series). London: Hodder Education, 2008, 208 pp.

Organisations

Chartered Institute of Personnel and Development (www.cipd.co.uk)

Chapter 3: Managing change and uncertainty

CMI management checklists

Implementing an effective change programme (Checklist 040)
Mapping an effective change programme (Checklist 038)
Understanding organisational culture (Checklist 232)

Other resources

Hartley, Jean, and others. *Leading with Political Awareness.* London: Chartered Management Institute and Warwick Business School, 2007, 72 pp.

Organisations

Chartered Institute of Personnel and Development (http://www.cipd. co.uk/subjects/corpstrtgy/changemmt)

Chapter 4: Managing stakeholders

CMI management checklists

Stakeholder analysis and management (Checklist 234)

Organisations

Investors in People (www.investorsinpeople.co.uk)
CMI ambassador programme (www.managers.org.uk/ambassadors)

Chapter 5: Managing risk

CMI management checklists

Business continuity (Checklist 151)

Other resources

Chartered Management Institute. *Management Futures: The World in 2018*. London: 2008, 26 pp.

Chartered *Management Institute. Risk Management: Guidance for Managers* (best practice guide). London: 2010, 8 pp.

Woodman, Patrick and Hutchings, Paul. *Disruption and Resilience: The 2010 Business Continuity Management Survey*. London: Chartered Management Institute, 2010, 28 pp.

Organisations

ALARM (www.alarm-uk.org/)

BSI Group – BS25999 Business continuity (www.bsigroup.com/en/Assessment-and-certification-services/management-systems/Standards-and-Schemes/BS-25999/)

Business Continuity Institute (www.thebci.org)

Institute of Risk Management (www.theirm.org)

UK Resilience (http://interim.cabinetoffice.gov.uk/ukresilience.aspx)

Chapter 6: Managing environment

CMI management checklists

Taking action on the environment (Checklist 019)

Other resources

Chartered Management Institute. *Environmental Management: Guidance for Managers* (best practice guide). London: 2009, 6 pp.

Wehrmeyer, Walter; and others. *Lean and Green: Leadership for the Low Carbon Economy*. London: Chartered Management Institute, 2009, 78 pp.

Organisations

Carbon Trust (www.carbontrust.co.uk)

Department for Environment Food and Rural Affairs (defra) (www.defra.gov.uk)

The Environment Agency (www.environment-agency.gov.uk)

Envirowise (http://envirowise.wrap.org.uk)

European Environment Agency (www.eea.europa.eu)

Chapter 7: Managing innovation

CMI management checklists

Understanding organisational culture (Checklist 232)

Other resources

Patterson, Fiona, and Maura Kerrin. *Innovation for the Recovery: Enhancing Innovative Working Practices*. London: Chartered Management Institute and NESTA, 2009, 31 pp.

Organisations

Department for Business Innovation and Skills (www.bis.gov.uk/innovation)

ideasUK (www.ideasuk.com)

Chapter 8: Managing reputation and brand values

Other resources

Brown, Michael and Turner, Paul. *The Admirable Company: Why Corporate Reputation Matters So Much and What it Takes to be Ranked Among the Best*. London: Profile Books, 2008, 248 pp.

Clifton, Rita; and others. *Brands and Branding*, 2nd edn. London: *The Economist* in association with Profile Books, 2009, 284 pp.

Griffin, Andrew. *New Strategies for Reputation Management: Gaining Control of Issues, Crises and Corporate Social Responsibility*. London: Kogan Page, 2008, 176 pp.

Honey, Gary. *A Short Guide to Reputation Risk*. Farnham: Gower, 2009, 119 pp.

Kapferer, Jean-Noel. *The New Strategic Brand Management: Creating and Sustaining Brand Equity Long Term*, 4th edn. London: Kogan Page, 2008, 560 pp.

Kornberger, Martin. *Brand Society: How Brands Transform Management and Lifestyle*. Cambridge: Cambridge University Press, 2010, 308 pp.

Reuvid, Jonathan. *Managing Business Risk: A Practical Guide to Protecting Your Business*. London: Kogan Page, 2008, 268 pp.

Organisations

British Brands Group (www.britishbrandsgroup.org.uk)

Chartered Institute of Management Accountants – corporate reputation (http://www.cimaglobal.com/en-gb/Thought-leadership/Research-topics/Marketing/Reputation--why-it-matters-and-how-you-can-manage-it11/)

Chapter 9: Diversity

CMI management checklists

Implementing a diversity management programme (Checklist 152)
Introducing an equal opportunities policy (Checklist 062)

Other resources

Chartered Management Institute. *Embracing Diversity* (best practice guide). London: 2007, 6 pp.

Chartered Management Institute, Institute for Employment Studies and Department for Work and Pensions. *Management Recruitment: Understanding Greater Routes to Diversity.* London: 2008, 25 pp.

Macleod, Alison, and others. *Managing an Ageing Workforce: How Employers are Adapting to an Older Labour Market.* London: Chartered Management Institute and Chartered Institute of Personnel and Development, 2010, 31 pp.

Organisations

ACAS – equality (www.acas.org.uk/index.aspx?articleid=1363)

Department for Business Innovation and Skills – Equality and Diversity toolkit (www.bis.gov.uk/policies/higher-education/access-to-professions/equality-diversity-toolkit)

Equality and Human Rights Commission (www.equalityhumanrights.com)

Government Equalities Office (www.equalities.gov.uk/news/equality_strategy.aspx)

National School of Government: Diversity Excellence model (www.nationalschool.gov.uk/organisational_development/Diversity/diversity_excellence_model/index.asp)